ANARCHY AT THE CIRCLE K

ON THE ROAD WITH
DEAD KENNEDYS, T.S.O.L.,
FLIPPER, SUBHUMANS,
AND... HEROIN

PATRICK O'NEIL

ANDREA:
PUBLISH THAT MEMOIR!

Patrick O'Neil

PUNK ✪ HOSTAGE ✪ PRESS

ANARCHY AT THE CIRCLE K
ON THE ROAD WITH
DEAD KENNEDYS, T.S.O.L.,
FLIPPER, SUBHUMANS,
AND... HEROIN

An imprint of Punk Hostage Press
ISBN: 978-1-940213-20-0

Foreword
Mia d'Bruzzi

Cover
Patrick O'Neil
Wat Todd

Punk Hostage Press
Hollywood, USA
www.punkhostagepress.com

For Wayne O'Neil

TABLE OF CONTENTS

FOREWORD

When my dear old friend Patrick asked me to read his new memoir, I thought great—he's a fantastic writer and I always enjoy reading his work. Little was I prepared for the shitstorm onslaught of memories his harrowing and truthful account would provoke in me. So, what to say? Yes—it's fucking accurate and it's a powerful, visceral, and realistic left hook of the reality of those days. All of these things took place, in the way Patrick describes, and it's an absolute miracle that he is still here to write about it. Reading it actually brings the taste of cheap booze, flat beer, bleach, and old cigarettes into my mouth—the flavor of load-in. My tinnitus attests to the decibel levels he describes at the shows— it's mine forever and I earned it. And the actual hustle it takes to be strung-out on the road requires the skills, endurance, and grit of a superhero mastermind evil genius. Patrick lived the life so you don't have to—just read his book and you will understand how it was.

–Mia d'Bruzzi, Frightwig

It's 1982. We're driving south on Highway 101 in Dead Kennedys' van. A golden brown and white Dodge Sportsman with the extended camper top. It's the kind of van an all-American dad would take on weekend camping trips. Except this one has been through a maelstrom of pain. It's the van from the apocalypse. Fucking Mad Max would have been proud to drive this van. There are dents, gouges, and rusty slices resembling machete hacks. If you were a serial killer abducting murder victims, this would be the vehicle you would use.

The back is packed with gear and we're heading to a gig at Foothill College in Los Altos Hills, California. On the bill opening for us tonight is a new band from Minnesota named Hüsker Dü. In the van with me are Microwave, Tracy Chick, and Chris Grayson. We're the road crew.

I have never set up a drum kit. I know nothing about sound, impedance, OHMs, mixing boards, or PAs. However, I do know how to tune a guitar. I can plug in an amp. I can drink a lot of beer and do whatever drugs are available. And I really don't seem to need sleep.

I'm a fucking roadie.

CALIFORNIA ÜBER ALLES
1983: DEAD KENNEDYS

The show is in a large warehouse storage facility aptly called Club Minimal. We're on the outskirts of Sacramento, or at least I think it's the outskirts. Having never been to Sacramento, I have no idea where we are, and I really don't care. But it is a storage facility in a fenced-in lot, the kind of drab nothingness where you'd expect to find a storage facility, and there isn't shit else around.

Dead Kennedys are here for two nights, and the opening lineup would be cool for any major city, but outrageously amazing for a small town like Sacramento. Tonight: Butthole Surfers, Tales of Terror, and Dead Pledge. Tomorrow: 7 Seconds, Straw Dogs, and Urban Assault. The promoter is a little annoying fuck named Stuart Katz. He yells a lot. I want to punch him. But then I want to punch a lot of people. So I just let it go and ignore the guy.

It's early evening, already dark, and we're late. We quickly load in. But first we check to make sure the band has beer, which means the crew has beer. The band: Jello Biafra (vocals), East Bay Ray (guitar), Klaus Fluoride (bass), and D.H. Peligro (drums), run through a quick sound check and then head to the motel. The crew stays with the gear.

"Dude, this isn't a club," I'm talking to Tracy, out front of the building by the van, and trying my best to sound like a seasoned pro. "It's a glorified fuckin' storage space."

"Never been here before?" Tracy knows I've never been here.

Even after working part time for the Kennedys for over a year, I'm still the FNG (Fucking New Guy). Tracy's primary mission in life is to give me shit. Only it's mostly good-natured and we're friends.

"Nah, dude. I don't hang out in shitholes like you do."

"Don't know what you're missing, *dude.*"

Tracy pulls out a can of black spray paint from under the van's passenger seat and starts tagging the wall of the club with his WIMPS moniker. Earlier Katz had given us the "no spray paint" lecture of keeping the building graffiti-free so he doesn't lose his lease, which apparently most of the bands have abided by. Only, a fresh unblemished wall is hard to pass up.

"Hey, throw up a D.K. Let 'em know we're here."

"Fuck that! Kennedys want their shit up? Let them do it. Like to see Biafra doing a little spraying now and then."

"Doubt that's gonna happen."

Club Minimal is one large room, cinder block walls, high vaulted ceiling, a plywood stage in the rear, and PA speakers on either side. The opening band whips through a quick set. Then it's Tales of Terror and Butthole Surfers. It's hot and sweaty and loud as hell. There's an urgency to get the bands on stage. Apparently, it's customary for the local cops to shut down Katz's shows.

"They're fuckin' brutal," he said.

The stage is small and barely off the pit, and by the time we go on it's a beer-drenched mess (never play after Butthole Surfers, they destroy stages). I'm over by Klaus's amp. I don't know it yet, but this will become my side of the stage for the next few years I'm working with the Kennedys. I can't really say why I prefer it to Ray's side, other than it just feels right.

Somewhere in my fifties I start heavily relying on the word "What?" I'm partially deaf and some people's voices just don't register. But hey, it's punk; I never considered wearing earplugs. It wasn't until I began working huge arena shows I noticed all the OG stagehands wore ear protection. Even then I thought they were wusses. Eventually I conceded looking uncool for a few hours was worth the tradeoff. If I hadn't, I'd probably be learning sign language.

There's a ton of stagedivers. If you can say nothing else about small town punks they are, at the very least, enthusiastic. The stage gets so crowded Biafra can't move. I grab the nearest kid dressed in the usual uniform of torn Levi's, cut-off band T-shirt, and combat boots, and toss him off into the crowd. Hopefully they will catch him or maybe just break his fall, but I'm already throwing the next kid off stage who is dressed so exactly alike I have to wonder if it's the same kid.

It's total chaos with all these punks on such a small stage, but I just keep throwing them off until there's room to move. An out-of-control stagediver sporting giant G.B.H. spikes, whirl-winding his arms as he runs across the stage, knocks over all the mic stands. Tracy catches him and the kid starts throwing punches. Tracy is not someone you want to get into a fight with. Born and raised in Wyoming with the name his mom gave him, Tracy Chick, could not have been an easy childhood. When he left town at sixteen and enlisted in the Navy, shit must have gotten worse. One thing Tracy excels at is beating the shit out of people. Not a big guy, just sort of wiry. He's quick and absolutely fearless. A lethal combination and a lot of wannabe hardcore dudes mistakenly think he's an easy fight.

Tracy has the kid in a headlock, and he's dragging him off stage behind the PA. He's going to kick the living shit out of the kid, making him regret he ever tried to punch anyone. I'm not really down with fucking people up. I can either get between them and possibly get smacked a few times in the process, or I can just let it go. Fuck, the kid started it, right?

I might be a tad angry, a little resentful, absolutely impulsive, and a whole lot of smartass. But unless I'm totally drunk or loaded on the right amount of drugs, I'm not as sure of myself in a fight as Tracy. I'm also not as jaded with experience. A few tours from now, Candace from Canada will tell me I'm the gentlest roadie she's ever seen. I get into fights only when I have to. This will change over the years, but for now I don't consider myself in the same "tough-guy" league with a lot of other roadies. I don't notch my belt by breaking faces, and I try to not get mine broke in the process.

I turn my attention back to the stage as an army of cops rush in the front door. Katz's security is against the wall as more cops shove their way farther into the room. A few have their batons out. The majority are arbitrarily grabbing punks and putting them up against the wall to be searched. A few are just needlessly destructive, aimlessly harassing people, and kicking over the merchandise table.

The house lights go on as everyone scrambles for the front door, leaving the pit empty and littered with debris. The band stops playing and Klaus tosses his bass in the air. It lands in the middle of the stage and feedbacks through the PA. The ensuing distortion reverberates throughout the room as we all walk away from the mayhem.

***

My life is going nowhere, and I don't know what I want to do. Nothing is fulfilling except getting loaded and hanging out at the clubs at night—and even that doesn't always cut it. Creating art used to be my entire focus. In 1979, I graduated from the San Francisco Art Institute with a bachelor's degree in film. I had entered art school as a printmaker, but my drawings had evolved from graphic imagery to complicated interpretations of movement and form that evolved into animation. Hence, the film degree.

My plan had always been to go to New York and follow my dreams becoming a comic book illustrator. Only art school hadn't prepared me for the real art world. The competition was brutal, and the established artists and publishers weren't very receptive or even welcoming. I didn't draw in what they considered the accepted traditional style and my story ideas were even less traditional. Being a naïve "fucking new guy" artist, I thought these guys would welcome me with open arms. What I got were snide comments regarding my artistic abilities and vague offers for long-term apprenticeship working for the "masters," which really meant glorified office boy and occasional penciler for unimportant titles and obscure projects.

After four years of being the hot-shit illustrator at art school, my inflated ego told me I was too good to waste my time running errands for arrogant prima donnas. Of course it didn't help I was using heroin and I was broke all the time. The reality of living in a cold water walk up in the Lower East Side, existing on cheap dope, pizza, Camel filters, and riding the subway everywhere for the next who knows how many years just wasn't that appealing. Plus it was New York City in the early '80s. Crime and drugs were everywhere. With my fondness for all things dark and seedy, I knew nothing about living in N.Y.C. was going to turn out well. Reluctantly, I packed up my portfolio, bruised ego, all my resentments, and went home defeated.

But in 1980, unemployed and career-less in San Francisco was no better. While New York's art scene was competitive, at least there was work to be had. In S.F., there was nothing but the occasional freelance job. One had to hustle hard to make a living and I just didn't have that drive. I was still resentful about my experience in New York, and deep down I felt ignored by the art world, or actually the world in general. If everyone could only see how talented I was, I'd be this famous "rockstar" artist. Pissed off, I stopped drawing and put all my energy into doing drugs.

Almost every morning I'd be lingering over a latte at Caffe Trieste in North Beach, bumming smokes from all the unemployed bohemians, and briefly scanning the want ads in the newspapers

other patrons had left behind. At night, I'd be at the Mabuhay
Gardens (The Mab) getting free drinks off Ike the bartender. Before
last call, I'd latch onto the closest woman and stay at her place. My
life was an endless routine of one-night stands, scrounging money
off friends, sleeping on couches, the occasional odd job, and barely
maintaining a heroin habit.

With nothing better to do, I co-founded an art noise band:
The Pillage People. Our objective was to create a barrage of noise
and our lineup changed with each show mainly due to depending on
who had instruments. Our first gig was at the Mab. The room was
packed, but we soon drove half the audience into the bar to get away
from our wall of noise. Those who did stay became part of the manic
whirlwind atmosphere where the line between the audience and
performers got totally blurred. Our unintended concept, born at that
first show, was to invite other musicians on stage from the audience
to join in or play our instruments, and then while "the band" was
playing, the original members would be at the bar drinking for free.

No matter how bad we actually were, being in a band helped
inflate my already inflated ego. Now I am a "rockstar." But the
minimum guarantee from the clubs did little for my financial
situation. Broke as fuck, I land a job stuffing envelopes for a horrible
vitamin corporation that later turned out to be a pyramid scheme. I
really hated my job and myself for working there. I'm drinking
heavily. I'm snorting a ton of speed and heroin. I'm arrogant and
abusive to everyone around me. I'm constantly getting in fights with
my girlfriend Brenda. I show up to work so loaded from the night
before that the days blur into one another.

I remember getting fired.

Or did I quit?

I'm standing outside the Mab smoking a cigarette. Some
fucked-up band is making noise inside, and I can't drink enough to
make them sound okay. I have a headache. I want to go home, but
I'm waiting for Brenda, which is stupid because we never leave until

after last call. Ike the bartender has been shoving drinks at me for hours. I feel like puking. It's probably midnight. But it could be later.

I'm talking with Microwave, Dead Kennedys' road manager, and we're both seriously drunk. I know Micro through Chris Grayson (my best friend, roommate, and whose ex-girlfriend Brenda is now my girlfriend). Chris, Brenda, and I live together in a one-bedroom apartment on Romolo Alley. It's weird and dysfunctional and we're all friends.

Microwave's asking if I know anyone he can hire to load gear for an upcoming Kennedys tour. I'm not really listening and then Chris comes out and joins us. Chris works sound at The Mab and for Dead Kennedys and TSOL when they tour. Across the street at The Stone, where all the heavy metal bands play, a bunch of long-legged girls in miniskirts and high heels are out front standing around with dorky dudes in spandex and lots of hair. I lean against The Mab's awning pole and wonder why those metal assholes get all the hot women who dress like hookers.

Chris and Microwave are arguing. I'm still not paying attention. I'm too wrapped up in feeling sorry for myself. I hate my life. I have nothing going on. I'm broke, existing on monthly unemployment checks, the occasional roadie gig, a lot of drugs and alcohol, and not getting much sleep.

"Wanna go on tour?" says Chris.

"Doin' what?" I ask. Like it actually makes a difference.

"Loading gear, working stage," says Microwave. "Shit you're already doin', Slick."

"Yeah, okay sure," I say, and then throw up in the gutter.

***

It's New Year's Eve 1983. Dead Kennedys are playing the Starlite Roller Rink in North Hollywood, California. Tonight at midnight we'll be venturing into Orwell's 1984. With the current political situation and the possibility that Reagan and his cronies with their plans for oppressive fiscal conservatism will soon be in power, Orwell's dystopian vision doesn't feel unrealistic.

The road crew drove all night to get here, although why I don't know. Microwave, the road manager, has a schedule reminiscent of a much older generation. He reasons that there's less traffic at 4AM so it's easier, but the lack of sleep from being up all night doesn't help, and the bright Los Angeles sunshine hurts my eyes.

Dead Kennedys picked up Microwave in Boston when they played Emerson College in '81. Or rather, Micro picked up the Kennedys when they played Emerson College, and he'd been with them ever since. Microwave's real name is Michael Bonanno, and its rumored he's related to the Bonanno crime family although Micro has never actually confirmed that rumor, and I always suspect he started it to give himself some street cred.

Unfortunately, with Micro calling the shots, the rift between him and Tracy is not getting any better. Tracy's distain for authority rubs Microwave the wrong way and he sees Tracy as not just a pain in the ass, but a liability. This will be Tracy's last out-of-town show working for the Kennedys. Tracy will never get outright fired. Instead, he just won't get the call to work the next tour.

Eight years later when I abruptly leave rehab, abandoning my first half-hearted attempt to get off heroin, Tracy will offer me a place to hide from my family, giving my junkie girlfriend Sara and me space to crash on the floor of his small San Francisco apartment while we scam our way back to Los Angeles. Eventually, Tracy and I will lose touch. Many years later, I'll hear he died of a ruptured pancreas at the age of 35. The first in the second wave of punks dying—no longer the drugs killing us—it's the aftermath of bad choices and even worse health.

It's only noon and a crowd of people are already hanging around the parking lot. There's something odd seeing punks in their leathers and spiked hair in daylight. The two just don't mix. Some L.A. punks even have tans, which in my fog-enshrouded San Francisco world is unheard of. But then Los Angeles is a strange scene and totally different than what I'm used to. The sheer intensity of the larger shows can be intimidating. There is always an underlying threat of violence.

The temporary stage, set up along the back wall of a large roller rink, crams the band up against the acoustic drop ceiling. East Bay Ray, the tallest of the Kennedys, has to play bent over during sound check or his head pushes on the low-hung acoustic ceiling panels.

T.S.O.L. and the Butthole Surfers are the opening lineup. It's a chaotic night, all the bands are super loud, there's a ton of feedback coming off the stage, and the crowd is exactly what most New Year's Eve crowds are—out of control and totally obnoxious. The Buttholes, still a bit unknown, totally kill it. This is the second time I've met all of them, and my first impression is they're strange and take a shitload of acid. Backstage they have sheets of windowpane and are slicing off multi-hit strips to take before the show. They're not doing this to impress anyone—this is just what they do. But the idea of tripping at a punk show sort of creeps me out.

T.S.O.L. rips through their set. Joe Wood howls his vocals, while Ron Emory puts out an intense wall of sound that seems impossible coming from one guitar. Mike Roche's bass is holding down the beat. This is a new version of T.S.O.L. Lead singer Jack Grisham and drummer Todd Barnes are no longer with the band, and the sound has changed to a more rock and roll edge. The lineup is the original members Mike Roche (bass) and Ron Emory (guitar/vocals) with new members Mitch Dean (drums), and Joe Wood (vocals/guitar). Later they'll go full metal, and their pervious hardcore punk audience will become disheartened with the direction the band is going. So will Mike and Ron. When they leave, the band will no longer have any original members.

By the time the Kennedys come on stage, the audience is pumped and New Year's Eve-loaded. Biafra launches himself at the mic totally pissed off. "Whoever stole a white pillowcase full of stuff out of the T-shirt room, please put it back. It has personal belongings like my contact lenses I use to see. They're of no value to you, but a hell of a lot of value to me. You can keep the D.I. records. Just give me back my stuff."

A kid at the front of the stage yells, "Fuck you, Biafra!" and the band launches into a cover of Johnny Paycheck's "Take This Job and Shove It." And they don't let up until the final refrains of "Moon Over Marin."

It's well past 1AM when we load out. It's warm for January, or at least a lot warmer than San Francisco. I'm wearing a T-shirt, no jacket, and the Valiums I took are kicking in. My ears are ringing and I'm physically tired. I lift Klaus's bass cabinet and slide it into the cargo area. D.H.'s trap case is falling apart, and Micro and Tracy struggle to keep it in one piece as they shove it into the back of the van. There's a rolling Anvil case for Ray's spare amp head and miscellaneous shit like cords and pedals that's so heavy I can't lift it, but Micro does with little effort. I'm self-conscious of how weak I am in comparison.

We all get in the van, with Micro at the wheel, and pull out of the parking lot. A platoon of L.A.P.D. in riot gear stand in front of their cars and paddy wagons, lined up like a gauntlet along either side of the street. An eerie red and white strobe from the multitude of flashing cop lights splashes on our faces and illuminates the interior of the van. We pass more cops and the carloads of punks pulled over for sobriety tests. A dude with a bright red mohawk is attempting to walk a straight line. A cop stands off to the side with a barking German Shepard on a leash. A motorcycle cop, complete with stormtrooper black leather boots and gold CHP helmet, waves us through. No one says anything until we make the freeway onramp.

***

We load-in at the Santa Cruz fairgrounds. The show is outdoors. The good weather has followed us north. There's a huge canvas awning over the stage as shade from the sun. It's another small-town shithole show. I don't know it then, but this will become the trademark for the majority of D.K. tours. More and more, we'll be playing so many out-of-the-way venues and podunk towns that we begin calling them "turd town" tours.

M.I.A., a melodic hardcore band from Las Vegas that never quite got the recognition they deserve, is on the bill with T.S.O.L. We're all hanging out backstage, drinking beers, and talking shit. Will Shatter from Flipper shows up. I've seen Flipper play a bunch of times, but I don't really know Will. Trying to be cool I say, "Hey Bruce, what's up?", mistaking him for Flipper's other singer Bruce Loose. Instead of being a dick, Will laughs and mumbles, "I'm Will." I'm embarrassed and Brenda makes it worse. "That's fucking Will Shatter, stupid." It's awkward, I feel self-conscious, and the rest of the night it doesn't get better.

The Kennedys are about to go on. I'm backstage picking up towels and bottled water. Will and Brenda are openly making out. My relationship with Brenda hasn't been going well. We're always fighting. I've cheated on her. She's probably cheated on me. But it still hurts my ego when she shoves it in my face and in front of the band and the crew. Yet, the karma of it all is oddly weird, as I did the same thing to Chris with Brenda. It's like some bad payback coming around and I deserve it.

At load-out, Will and Brenda are gone. I leave on tour with T.S.O.L. the next day. I never live with Brenda again. We never talk about it.

A year from now, Chris and I will be on tour with the Kennedys. Our conversation will somehow veer off into the women we've been with, and the subject of Brenda and Will Shatter will come up, and I'll jokingly say, "She's crazy. The best thing that ever happened was her leaving me for Will. In fact, I owe Will for getting her out of my life, and really you owe me for the same thing." Chris will get silent and bristle with anger. "I don't owe you anything," and I'll realize just how hurt he'd been when Brenda left him for me. I'll feel like a total piece of shit.

CHANGE TODAY?
1984: T.S.O.L.

"That'll need stitches." The nurse is staring at the deep cut in my hand as a rivulet of blood runs down my bare arm and drips onto the linoleum floor. We're in the emergency room, which looks like every other emergency room in America, but this is Denver and some skinhead just sliced me with a razor.

After wrapping my hand with a large temporary dressing to stop the blood flow, the nurse reaches over and turns my head.

"Let me see your face."

She wants to examine my black eye. Only that's not why I'm here. The cut is a lot more urgent, or at least to me it is, because I can't stop the bleeding.

"Don't worry about it. That's from last night. Fix this instead." I hold up my bandaged hand to ward her off, so she'll stop touching me. I'm embarrassed enough about the shiner.

Last night in Salt Lake City, two jocks jumped me in the back stairwell of the Indian Center. I was trying to stop a fight between a little punk girl and some large dude that must have been their friend. When he swung at the girl, I grabbed his arm and then all I remember is being slammed backwards into the concrete wall and getting repeatedly punched in the face. I was going down, sliding to the floor, almost unconscious. I kicked out as hard as I could—my steel-toed boot connecting with a knee—and he backed off.

"Last night?" A doctor is now standing next to the nurse. They're both looking at me as if I'm some undiscovered species. "You get in a lot of fights?"

How do I answer that? I work onstage during the show when the band plays. It's punk. The audience continually assaults the stage for a few seconds of hang time. Some grab the mic and shout along to the lyrics. Most do a pantomime of the Circle Jerks' skanking kid and then dive off the stage. When they don't get off or crash into the gear knocking shit over, I throw them back into the crowd. Some don't go willingly. Punches are thrown. Is that really a fight?

"I'm on tour. Shit like this happens."

This tour isn't going well for me. We played Seattle a few nights ago and my leather jacket was stolen. It's Fall in the Northwest and I'm freezing. Then we hit Salt Lake and I get the shit kicked out of me. Thankfully nothing happened in Eugene or Reno. But I'm worried the band is thinking I'm a liability. Their manager, Mike Vraney, is eyeing me like I have the dark cloud of doom hanging over me—he's bad juju, man.

Tonight, we're playing Denver and there's a ton of skins in the audience. I'm no stranger to dealing with skinheads. Working stage and security at The Mab and the On Broadway in San Francisco, I'm constantly getting into altercations, especially with skinheads and their penchant for violence and rat pack mentality. There's also a conflict with our political beliefs. I don't fucking like racist Nazis.

A group of skinheads at the front of the stage keep fucking with the mic stands. Every time Ron steps up to sing, they shove it and the mic smashes him in the mouth. They laugh when they do it and they're pissing me off. I leap into the audience and push a large skinhead back away from the stage—and then after getting elbowed and kicked by the others—I hit him in the head. A short, stocky skinhead in a spiked leather lunges at me from the side. I shove him out of the away as they all oddly keep their distance.

Back up on stage and I right the mic stand. But there's blood everywhere. It's splattered on my boots and all over the stage. I check my arms and hands and there's a long thin slice from my thumb to my wrist with blood spurting out at a scary rate. The skinheads are laughing. The short, stocky one smiles and waves.

I find the promoter; he grabs one of his guys. "Drive this dude to the emergency room, now!" As we're pushing through the crowd, I run into Jello Biafra. The expression on his face confirms that I look like a fucking mess. "You okay?" he asks, eyeing my bloody hand and black eye. "Want me to take you to the hospital?"

"No, I got this."

"So... what's being on tour mean?" The doctor has cleaned the blood off my hand and scrubbed the cut for possible foreign objects. With a looping movement, he uses a circular needle and begins stitching the wound closed.

"Every night the band plays a different city. I drive. I load gear. I work the stage. Sometimes there's a fight."

"And you get paid to do that?"

"Yeah."

"Maybe you should find another line of work?"

That is the reaction a lot of people have outside of the punk scene. They don't really understand punk, and they definitely don't get touring. They either think I'm driving around the country for free, or I'm an irresponsible drug addict who found a way to avoid getting a real job and won't grow up. Although both of those statements may be true to an extent—especially the working for free comment—what they really don't understand is this isn't just a job; it's also my life and my identity. I'm not punk for the day. I don't buy my band T-shirts already torn and cut up at a mall. In fact, I hardly ever wear band T-shirts (especially not the bands I work for), but that's beside the point. A friend from art school asked me if I liked punk and the reality is that I never even thought about it, it's just what I do. It's about finding your tribe and I had finally found mine.

The doctor is done sewing me up.

"It's going to be a little stiff for a few days. Try not to use your hand. Don't lift anything heavy. In two weeks, come back, get the stiches taken out."

"What about the pain?"

The doctor squints over his glasses. "I'm not comfortable giving you pain medication."

"I'm not comfortable being in pain."

A few minutes of handwringing and the doctor writes a prescription for codeine, which is the equivalent of throwing a shot glass of water at a raging house fire. I'm strung-out on heroin. I've got better drugs in the van. I don't even bother to fill the prescription in the pharmacy before leaving the hospital.

The promoter's guy is waiting for me outside the ER. I light a cigarette and tell him I want to go back to the show. My overly bandaged hand looks worse than it actually is.

"Damn, dude. You're like a warrior, man."

"Shut the fuck up."

LOS ANGELES
1984: BUENA PARK

While I was away on tour, Brenda moved Will Shatter into our North Beach apartment. Not that I was planning on getting back together with her. It's just a stark reminder I have nowhere to actually call home. Chris convinces me to stay in Los Angeles, or more specifically in Orange County where he lives. "I'll hook you up, there's a ton of work."

I have never really considered living in Southern California other than having a minor epiphany at a Taco Bell while eating a burrito one morning after a show in Hollywood. I was outside sitting at a table, groggy from lack of sleep and too many Darvons from the night before. It was sunny and warm. I realized the weather was like this all year round. San Francisco is always cold—especially in the summer—and that morning I had the thought, *I could live here.*

The idea of returning to S.F. and scrambling to find a place to live sucks. I'm embarrassed Brenda dumped me for Will. Chris lives with Mike Vraney, and they agree to let me stay with them temporarily. It's just the living room couch, so I'm not that stoked. After a particularly tedious all-night coke binge, the two of them teeth grinding and tweaking, my nerves and lungs are totally shot. With no heroin to come down with, I want to blow my brains out. I need a room of my own where I can hide.

Gerry Hurtado (Skatemaster Tate or just plain Taters) offered me a vacant room in his house in Buena Park and I take it. Yet, the depressing reality of moving away from San Francisco hits home that first night. I'm in a nondescript room, in a nondescript tract house, in a nondescript subdivision of a nondescript suburb. I'm in culture shock. I have never lived anywhere as remotely ordinary. It's depressing.

Earlier that night, Taters and I had hit In-N-Out Burger and eaten double-doubles, fries, and chocolate shakes. In the parking lot, dudes with hotrods, tripped out Camaros, and lowered Impalas revved their motors. Women were hanging around in small packs. They all looked like cheerleaders. Everyone was either blonde-haired, blue-eyed, and tanned, or Latina and badass. All the dudes had bad tattoos, and the prevailing fashion was either rockabilly or cholo-cool. Dressed in black jeans, motorcycle boots, and a cut-off T-shirt, I felt like the new kid the first day of high school.

It's midnight. I'm alone in bed staring at the textured stucco popcorn ceiling wondering if I've made a huge mistake. Other than the guys in T.S.O.L. and Taters, I don't know anyone. Forever feeling like an outsider, I'll struggle with a sense of belonging. In a room full of people, I'll feel alone.

2012. I get a message from Gerry through social media. We hadn't talked in years. After a quick, "How the hell are you?" we tried to make plans to meet up in person. I'd say, "Hey, I'm going to this event, are you?" and he'd say, "Shit, I can't make it, how about we meet at this show…" but I'd have previous commitment and we'd say, "Okay, another time then." I always thought we had all the time in the world. October 13, 2015, I got news Taters had died of cancer. He was fifty-six years old. Taters's death hit hard. I made a vow to always make time to see old friends. Nothing in this world is permanent.

The next day blurs into more days and then weeks of the sameness. Without a car I'm stuck at Taters's. Occasionally, Chris and Ron Emory come over and drag me outside into the sunshine. We drive to a canal or a pool or some skating spot and go at it in the heat for hours. Ron is a killer skateboarder, which intimidates me. I suck and usually end up frustrated, give up, and wait in the shade while comparing myself to the other skaters—all of them tanned with perfect physiques, lean and muscular. I'm pasty-faced, white with freckles and dyed black hair. No matter how skinny I get, I don't have a flat washboard stomach. I don't tan. I don't wear shorts. I can't swim. I don't surf. Even though my experience with skateboarding is that it's for rebels. In SoCal, it feels like a competitive sport. After a few attempts to get me to skate, Chris and Ron stop picking me up. I begin avoiding the outside and sleep most of the day.

Fortunately, everyone stops by Taters's so I can't completely isolate. Tater knows every musician and drug addict in Orange County. There's always something happening: a show to go to, or drugs to be done. Taters and his friends don't use needles. They smoke or snort or take pills. I don't want to be the odd man out, but pills take too long, smoking heroin is a waste, and I don't snort anything anymore. When I score dope, I usually retreat to my room. I probably seem stuck-up and standoffish. I'd rather mainline my drugs and nod out alone than use them like an amateur just to be social.

When the month is up, I pack my bag and head north to San Francisco. The devil you know is sometimes better.

Six years later, I'll move back to L.A. after living in New York for a year trying to get off heroin. Anna Lisa and I will continue a long-distance relationship, but really, I'm just cheating on her and not being honest about it. I'll hook up with Chris and get a job working stage for Kevin Lyman at Goldenvoice. I'll rent a room from Debbie Gordon in Silver Lake and slowly fall back into my old habits—drinking a fifth of booze every night, then chipping away with the occasional hit of heroin. When I get a good dope connection, I stop drinking altogether.

Once again, I'm strung-out and need a hustle. Chris and I start selling heroin to all the musicians and punks we know in Hollywood. Our pager goes off non-stop and our clientele grows. A year and a half later, Chris is murdered in a drug deal gone bad. A drug deal I should have been at with him. I identify his body at the morgue. The cops question me about his murder, but it's overly apparent they don't give a shit about solving this crime. It's just another dead drug dealer in Los Angeles.

I drag myself to the valley and attend Chris's wake. All the Red Hot Chili Peppers are there, the road crew, T.S.O.L., and a host of other bands and musicians Chris did sound for and I don't really know. Chris's mom is also there. It's my first time meeting her. I tell her I'm sorry. Everyone else I avoid. Not long after, I head back to S.F. and life gets much worse.

In 2009, with eight years clean off drugs, I move back to Los Angeles. I live in the exact same drug-infested shithole neighborhood in Hollywood that I left in '91.

EVER FALLEN IN LOVE (WITH SOMEONE YOU SHOULDN'T'VE) 1984: SAN FRANCISCO

The return home is anticlimactic. I've no place to live and no tour anytime soon. All I own is a bag of clothes and a Fender bass. After a week of couch surfing, I get restless. I need to do what I usually do: meet a girl at a club, go home with her, have sex, then move in. I'm hanging out with a couple of different women, but I'm not serious about any of them.

Kat is a professional rock and roll groupie. She's tight with all the metal dudes and get passes for huge arena shows like Judas Priest and AC/DC. Kat buys a lot of coke and even though I hate coke, I do it with her. When she's thoroughly gacked, she likes to give me head. When I come, she gags and makes a big production of spitting my jizz into a towel. This makes me totally self-conscious. I'm wondering if this is her normal routine, or is it just my cum that's so offensive? Kat claims to have sucked a million rockers' cocks and, in her rock and roll world, I guess that's something to brag about. I find it sort of sad. *Does she spit out their cum too?*

One night in a moment of vulnerability Kat confides that she used to be overweight, showing me the stretch marks on her boobs, and then explains how it all changed when she found drugs and rock and roll. "They saved my life." There's a strange lost child quality to her when she's not putting up a hard front. Shit like her bed is covered with stuffed animals and she sleeps with them all.

Then, just as quickly, she switches back to groupie mode and demands to give me head. Yet the pleasure from getting a blowjob is overshadowed by all the gagging afterwards. It's so weirdly repulsive I can't take it and start making excuses—trying to avoid the whole uncomfortable scene.

On the nights I have nowhere else to go, I lose my resolve and stay with her. This leads to a few nights where I just don't want to have sex, which is something she can't fathom, and we argue. Plus Kat's anti-needles and her new routine is to lecture me about the dangers of shooting drugs. The last night I stay with her, she asks me to promise I'll never do it again. Of course I say yes, and then the next morning I fix in her bathroom while she's at her day job. I feel guilty I'm using her for a place to sleep. I stop calling and disappear.

Siobhan is gorgeous. She's Japanese, Black, and Irish. She's stick thin and looks like a model. When we have sex, our hip bones collide, and I have bruises for days afterwards. Siobhan sort of attaches herself to me. I'm not sure what we're doing together. She lives in a tiny back room of a Victorian in the Mission that's so small her bed fills up the entire space. She lives on nothing and eats even less. I want to shoot dope and nod out for days in her little room. But her roommates, the ones who actually pay the rent, aren't happy she's got someone living with her, especially a junkie, and before she gets kicked out, I move on.

Anna Lisa's got a boyfriend Sean. He's the bass player for The Fuck-Ups. But that doesn't stop Anna Lisa and me from flirting backstage at shows. Michelle Rebel, bartender at the On Broadway, tells me Anna Lisa has a crush on me.

"She's got a boyfriend," I say.

The night Anna Lisa and I make plans to go out, she's been in a skateboarding accident and shows up with two black eyes and a neck brace. We end up fucking at her place. Anna Lisa lives at Mission A, a former boarding house on Mission Street that will later be known in some circles as "the Flipper house" because Flipper's drummer Steve DePace lives there as well. Anna Lisa's ten years younger than me. She cuts hair at Vidal Sassoon and skates with the YAA Girlz (Young Alluring Alcoholics). We go to a lot of shows. We fuck a lot. We do a lot of drugs. I move my meager belongings into her room at Mission A.

I think I'm in love.

WHERE'S THE FREEDOM?
1984: SUBHUMANS

Dick Lucas, lead singer for Subhumans, never liked the word "manager." Even tacked onto "road manager," it still freaked him out. Like his Crass roots were showing and they were going to take his punk card away for selling out. I guess anarcho-punks weren't supposed to make money, and nothing said establishment more to Dick than having anything close to the traditional definition of management. Every time I introduced myself as Subhumans' road manager, he'd flinch. He preferred to call me their driver. And I guess I was as none of them had a driver's license or even knew how to drive.

This was 1984 and Subhumans (not to be confused with the Canadian punk band Subhumans) lineup was Dick Lucas (vocals), Bruce Treasure (guitar), Phil Bryant (bass), and Trotsky (drums). At 23, Dick was the oldest member of the band. Me being the eldest at 29, I'm immediately dubbed Uncle Patrick.

Subhumans flew into San Francisco from England with a guitar, bass, a few sets of drumsticks, and Pete the Roadie—a roadie who had no idea which end of the guitar cord to plug in or where to plug it. The deal was we were going to borrow gear for every show. Which meant someone had to arrange that. Which also meant someone had to get them to the show, get them up on stage, pour beer in their mouths, let them play, get paid, pack them back up, feed them a veggie roll or two, and drive them to the next venue. That was the routine, over and over again, across the entire United States for the next month and a half, and that's exactly what I signed up to do.

Mike Vraney, T.S.O.L.'s manager, had booked the tour. John Loder—producer and studio engineer for Crass, and manager for Subhumans—had hired me as road manager, and now Pete the Roadie and I were all they had.

Three days in and we're in Pasadena at Perkins Palace. Youth Brigade, M.I.A., and Doctor Know are on the bill, and it's a fucking madhouse. Dick's upset. He's got me on the side of the stage and he's pointing at the bouncers tossing off punks—some landing on their heads in the middle of the pit.

"They're fuckin' killin 'em."

"And?" I say.

"Can't be doin' that durin' our set."

"Let me see what I can do."

Dream is running the stage crew for Gary Tovar, and he just looks at me vacant, like I'm speaking in tongues. Hell, it's business as usual. Just another Goldenvoice show in L.A. with a bunch of suburban punks who have traded in football for stagediving, and it's controlled mayhem at its best. Dream and his crew are just doing what they do.

"Talk to Tovar," he says.

Gary Tovar *is* Goldenvoice. He's put on most of L.A.'s major punk events and helped a lot of bands along the way. When I finally find Tovar backstage, I try to explain Dick's concerns about the bouncers. The opening band is so fucking loud I have to yell, and Tovar thinks I'm getting in his face.

"Hey, this ain't San Francisco," yells Gary. "This is fucking L.A."

Gary's dig is that I'm from San Francisco and we're pussies, or something along those lines, but definitely not the hardcore of L.A. This has been an ongoing rivalry since the dawn of West Coast punk, and its fucking tiresome, but what the hell. I'm not here to set the record straight.

"Just have your crew knock it down a notch while we're playing."

"Those kids get on my stage, they're treated like adults. Can't act right, they get tossed off."

I find Dick in the maze of dressing rooms backstage. It's dark and dank, the rooms empty, the floors littered with debris. Reminds me of a New York shoot gallery. Dick is talking to a guy who claims to run a video company. He wants to film Subhumans and he's asking for a signed release.

"We shot Flipper's bootleg video," he proudly says.

"Seen that," I say. "It sucks."

"Who the fuck are you?"

"His road manager." I say, pointing at Dick as he squirms.

"No, no, no, he's not," shouts Dick.

"You don't have permission to shoot no fuckin' video."

"But Uncle Pat, I loved that Flipper vid."

"Do not fuckin' sign anything," I yell.

The scumbag video dude is shooting daggers with his eyes. A girl in the next room screams and two glue-heads, looking guilty as sin, come hauling ass and run into us, knocking me over. I pull myself up off the floor, self-conscious that I got dumped on my ass by a couple of huffers. Scumbag video dude and Dick are gone. I'm sure Dick is going to do the über punk thing and sign away his rights so scumbag video dude can shoot with impunity and keep whatever measly profits there are for himself.

"Shit." I didn't promise John Loder anything more than I'd get them safely through the tour and then onto a plane home.

I light a cigarette as a four-foot-tall girl with a blue double mohawk, leather jacket, Exploited T-shirt, red tartan Catholic schoolgirl skirt, torn fishnets, and Doc Martens stumbles into me.

"Don't I know you?"

"Hard to say. There's at least ten of you at every show."

***

Driving Interstate 80, doing ninety, pushing it to get to Salt Lake City. We're dropping down into one parched valley after another parched valley in a string of parched valleys. It's desolate, like a moonscape or some destroyed country after an atomic bomb. I've never understood Utah. I mean I understand it as a piece of land. But what I don't understand is why the hell anyone would live here.

We're a half hour west of Salt Lake City, passing a submerged amusement park off the shore of the Great Salt Lake. So eerily strange the minarets of a castle barely sticking out of the water, next to the skeleton of some rollercoaster ride. Sums up everything I think of Utah. Another mindless entertaining thing to do mangled and destroyed. Like this Mormon-run state is just hell bent on stopping anything even remotely fun.

The Interstate is divided by a large expanse of scraggly desert grass. A white car on the westbound lane crests the hill and veers into the median on a crash course straight towards us.

"What the fuck's with that?"

Dick has a quizzical look on his face. I notice his glasses need cleaning as usual. We're all crammed into the minivan. Everyone else is asleep. The white car is thirty feet away. The driver and the passenger are wearing cowboy hats. There's a beehive emblem and "Highway Patrol" across the door, but no light bar on the roof.

I slow down, but it's too late. The cops turn on their siren, fishtailing sideways across two lanes, riding on the shoulder, and then flooring it to catch us. Seems like a lot of effort just for speeding. Instead of making them chase us, I pull to the shoulder and wait.

"Know why I'm stopping you?" The cop is out of breath like he was running, but he's only walked ten feet to stand outside my window.

"Because I was speeding?"

"Where you headed?"

"Salt Lake."

"Not going to make it if you keep this up. How you want to plead?"

"Plead? Don't you just give me a ticket I pay when I get home?"

"Not when you're doing thirty miles over the speed limit. I could take you to jail. Y'all have to see the judge."

The courtroom isn't so much a courtroom as it is an office. I'm talking to a woman behind a glass partition, the kind check-cashing places have where there's a hole to speak through and a slot at counter level where they hand you money. I push the ticket the cop gave me through the slot in the glass.

"Your Honor? Got a speeder!" she yells.

"How fast?" A man's voice echoes from the other room.

"Ninety-two." The woman behind the counter smiles. The corner of her eyes crinkle up.

"Ooh-wee, that's gonna cost 'em."

An old guy with gray hair and a heavy paunch comes out of the back office, hitching his pants up. He gives me the once over and then leans on the counter next to the woman.

"In a hurry, were ya? That's a two-hundred-and-seventy-five dollar fine. Paid now. In full."

I pull out our meager wad of cash and start to count. Flattening the twenties and tens, I take my time. The old guy and woman watch as I straighten the ratty bills. The promoter from the show last night paid me in small denominations. It's not a pretty pile of money.

"Here. Two. Seventy. Five." I say and pass the tattered pile of bills through the slot.

The woman picks them up as if they were contaminated.

"Need a receipt for that."

"Oh, you'll get your receipt," says the old guy. "Just driving through?"

"Yeah, heading east."

Subhumans are lounging on the lawn in front of the courthouse. The two cops are standing by their patrol car.

"Get in the van," I say.

"I'm hungry," says Trotsky.

"We're not stopping until we get the fuck outta Utah."

* * *

It was a strange noise. Couldn't really tell you what it was, but it woke me up. Sort of a resounding thud, and then being slightly awake, I hear muffled screams through the walls. They were close—next room over, or maybe farther down. The noise doesn't appear to have woken anyone else. I sit up in bed, lean against the wall, and feel it cool on my bare back. I need sleep, only now there's sirens in the distance getting closer, added to the screaming keeping me awake. Flashing red lights illuminate the curtains. Tires screech on asphalt followed by the squawk of police radios. I get out of bed and pull on some clothes.

A dozen cop cars, a couple ambulances, and a fire truck are parked haphazardly across the parking lot. Men in uniform are running past as I close the door behind me. The cops have a tall Black man in cuffs, leading him toward a patrol car. He's dressed in only a wife-beater and boxer shorts. He's barefoot and there's ice on the ground. I'm thinking he's got to be cold. I can see my breath as I fumble for a cigarette.

A crowd of cops and paramedics stand in a doorway four doors down the line of rooms from ours. We're in one of those motor court motels: a flat one-story building with a parking space in front of each room.

There's a gurney and paramedics outside the room. But the cops are in the way—just standing and waiting.

"What happened?" I ask a fireman.

"Pimp shot a hooker."

I'm thinking, *We're in Salt Lake City. This is Mormon country. Didn't even know they had pimps or hookers.*

"She dead?"

"She ain't gonna be running no marathon."

I have to drive the band to Denver. We've a show and then we're heading to Kansas City.

A cop walks up and stands next to the fireman. "How's it going, Frank?"

"Shot at her three times with a .45. Missed twice, but one of 'em took her head off."

"That can't be pretty to look at."

My cigarette is burned down to the filter. I drop it to the ground and put it out with the toe of my boot.

"What're you doin' here?" The cop is staring—noticing me for the first time.

"I'm in room eleven."

"Well then get back to room eleven."

It's dark and warm inside. None of the guys are awake. I go into the bathroom to take a piss. Turning on the light, I notice chunks of plaster on the floor. Above the toilet there's a four-inch hole. On the facing wall, another smaller hole where the bullet must have continued on. If I'd been standing where I am now when he pulled the trigger it would've gone right through me.

***

Last night we played the Foolkiller club in Kansas City. Bruce met a girl who was in the process of moving out of her apartment and she just hands us the keys, saying we could stay there. The band is sitting around the vacant living room on the bare hardwood floors.

"Wanna go to the club?" I ask. And everyone ignores me. The Dicks are playing at the venue we played last night. I figure we get in for free and drink their beer, which is a definite plus as we have no money.

The van is parked on the street by the Kansas City Art Institute and there are a lot of trendy artist types out on the street. They look like clean-cut nerds—like David Byrne from Talking Heads.

"Where are we?" asks Dick.

"Kansas City."

"And what happens here?"

"Mobsters get massacred and they slaughter a lot of cows."

"That's barbaric."

Debbie Gordon, The Dicks' manager, is getting out of their van as we pull up outside the club. "Saw y'all played here last night," she says. "Thought you'd be on the road by now."

"Night off. Came down to see you guys."

"Cool, but you're not drinking all our beer."

"Of course not."

The band follows Debbie into the club and I stay out front, light a cigarette, and lean against a brick wall. It's warm, the weather unseasonably mild for this time a year, and I'm grateful for a few minutes alone. A small girl with ratted, messed up hair, Doc Martens, and a studded leather jacket is standing a few feet away. There's a smirk on her face and she's coming my way.

"My name's Patti Mitchell," she says and hands me the open tall can of Pabst Blue Ribbon she's hidden under her jacket. I pull out my small bag of Valiums and wash down a couple with a chug of beer.

I wake up in a bedroom. Not just any bedroom. It's a little girl's bedroom, with Echo & The Bunnymen and Duran Duran posters on the walls. There're cute stuffed animals, a Hello Kitty bedspread, and a framed picture of a baby monkey dangling from a tree limb with "hang in there" written across the bottom. There's also a studded leather jacket and Doc Martens on the floor mixed with my clothes.

I'm under the covers, naked, wondering how I got here, and what the fuck happened last night. I don't know where the band is. I don't like to let them out of my sight. I remember we had a night off. We went to a club to see The Dicks. I remember saying hi to Gary Floyd and talking with Debbie while drinking PBRs backstage. But that's where my memories end.

I lie immobile, staring at the ceiling. I hear noises. People talking. A distant clanking of pots and pans like someone's in the kitchen. There's a shower running somewhere. I think I hear a radio. I'm getting nervous. I don't want to get up. I'm afraid to go out of the room. My head is splitting. I need drugs. I need a cigarette. I've got to take a piss.

There's a window next to the bed. I reach over and push back the curtain. Outside there's a lawn and trees and bushes and no buildings. I'm in the fucking country. I hate the fucking country. I'm really nervous now.

I grab my pants and search the pockets until I find three Valiums in a small Ziploc baggie. Thank god I didn't do them all last night. I look around but there's nothing to drink. I try to conjure up some spit. I've got cottonmouth so bad there is none and I dry swallow the pills. Stuck in my throat, they start to dissolve and taste like shit. But they're in me. They can melt on my tongue for all I care. I just want them to work, to take the edge off.

I'm searching my leather jacket for cigarettes when the door opens. A cute girl comes in drying her hair with a towel. She looks to be about sixteen. I'm hoping she's at least eighteen.

"You're finally up," she says.

"Hey," I say, checking her out, trying to remember who she is. And then, after failing, to avoid feeling any more awkward, I ask, "What time is it?"

"It's ten in the morning," she says. "It's awfully late for Patti Mitchell to be getting up."

"Who the fuck is Patti Mitchell?"

"I'm Patti Mitchell," she says and slumps on the end of the bed. Her eyes moist like she's about to cry.

"Sorry, I'm no good with names. Sorta slow in the morning."

Patti Mitchell perks up and smiles. "That's okay. You hungry?"

"Could use a cigarette." I reach for my pants and stand to put them on. I can feel her watching while I grab my T-shirt. The fucking shirt smells like sweat and beer. But what choice do I have—so I slip it over my head.

"Where are we?" I ask.

"My house," says Patti.

"Your house," I repeat and then feel better. Like possibly this is her house and maybe she has roommates who are out there doing things that roommates do.

"Where's your house?"

"Shawnee Heights. Shawnee Heights, Kansas."

I have no fucking idea where Shawnee Heights, Kansas is. I was in Kansas City, Missouri last night. I'm wondering if I drove here. I'm wondering if I've driven an underage girl across state lines. I'm wondering if we had sex. I'm thinking we did. I'm afraid to ask.

"Did I drive here?"

"Yeah. You were so wasted, amazed you could drive."

Now I'm feeling better. I have the van. I can escape.

"Come on. I'm hungry. Let's go eat," says Patti.

"There a restaurant nearby?" I'm hoping we can get out of here and head back to find the band.

"Don't need a restaurant. Mom's cooking."

I'm suddenly very nervous, and then the Valiums kick in.

The hallway is dark, there's deep pile green shag carpet and wallpaper with big pink flowers. I see the bathroom and tell Pattie I got to take a piss. But don't go anywhere. Don't leave me alone.

The bathroom is blue. I mean every-fucking-thing is blue: tiles, walls, towels, even the goddamn hand soap. There're some blue doily-ass curtains, and one of those annoying carpeted toilet seat covers that you have to hold up or else it'll fall down mid-piss.

I check myself in the mirror. I'm a fucking mess. My hair is all over the place, sticking out in different directions. There's darkness under my eyes. I look gaunt, but I like that. Last night was the first real sleep I've had in weeks.

I lift the blue-carpeted toilet seat and take a piss. The stench of my unwashed body envelops the room, killing the air freshener. I could use a shower. Instead I run some water in the sink, splash my face, and spike my hair with the blue liquid hand soap.

The hallway's empty, Patti is gone. I hear noises at the end of the hall, there's people talking. I think I hear Patti's voice. I walk into the kitchen. A woman stands at the stove frying sausages. She's wearing skintight leopard print capris, a frilly apron, and high heels. Her hair's big, ratted out, and bleached blonde. A tough-looking older guy sits at the kitchen table reading a newspaper. A cigarette dangles from his lips and he doesn't even look up or acknowledge

I'm there. Next to him is a kid in a football jersey. He's clocking me heavy. I nod. He sneers. Patti is nowhere to be seen.

The woman turns with the frying pan in her hand. "Oh, you must be Patti's friend," she says, and everyone looks me up and down. "You hungry?" she asks, the spatula poised in midair.

"I could use a cigarette."

"Hank," the woman yells. "Give Patti's friend a cigarette."

Hank lowers his paper. He looks like a cop, or a DEA agent. He's a fucking bad ass, or at least he used to be. "Here." He tosses me a pack of Marlboros. I fucking hate Marlboros. But what the hell.

"Got a light?" I pull one free of the pack. He slides a brass Zippo my way and I spark up. When I push the lighter back, I notice *Semper Fi* etched in its side.

"Sit," says the woman, indicating a chair at the table. I reluctantly take a seat by sneering boy. I'm wondering what I've gotten myself into. Is this some sort of demented *Leave It to Beaver* sitcom? And where the hell is Patti?

"You in a band?" asks sneering boy.

"Work for a band," I say, and notice dad as he raises an eyebrow.

"What do ya mean work for a band?" says dad.

"I'm a road manager. I manage bands while they're on tour."

"You make money doing that?"

"I make a living," I say flicking the cigarette ash in the ashtray.

"How much is 'making a living'?" he says and looks at me all intense.

I have to think about this. Like how much do I really make? Somewhere around three hundred a week. Which barely pays for a maintenance heroin habit. I also buy a lot of pills. Then there's the occasional speed for the all-night drives and bad food at truck stops. But I don't really live anywhere. I don't have to pay rent. I drink free at the clubs. My overhead is sort of low.

"Thirty thousand a year," I lie.

The dad's expression changes. He looks more relaxed, like he's seeing me from a new perspective. Like I'm no longer just a scumbag punk at his breakfast table. A scumbag punk that banged his teenage daughter and is smoking his cigarettes. Nope. Now I'm a scumbag punk who makes bank.

"Got a beer?" I ask.

"Beer?" says the mom.

"Breakfast of champions."

The kid snorts and says, "Losers you mean, don't ya?"

The kid is obviously a jock and the type of guy I hated in high school. Well, at least the type of guy I got in fights with when I actually went to high school. I want to smack him. But, really, I just want to leave. I want to run outside screaming in fear. This is so fucking uncomfortable. Where the hell is Patti Mitchell and why did she leave me here to deal with this all alone?

Mom takes out a longneck Budweiser from the fridge and hands it to me. I twist the top off and take a swig. The beer hits my stomach hard. The first beer of the day always does.

In a flurry of domestic activity, mom serves up plates of eggs, fried potatoes, and sausages. When she lays a plate down in front of the empty chair by her husband, she calls out for Patti to come to the table, food's ready.

Patti runs in through the backdoor. There's a dog following her. It scurries across the room to sniff my crotch and then disappears down the hallway. I look at my plate of food and know I can't eat it. Patti sits down and grabs a piece of toast off the stack on a plate in the middle of the table and starts slathering red jam all over it. I try to catch her eye, but she's not looking at me. I'm wondering does Patti bring home a lot of scumbag punks? I mean they're all too relaxed about this. What the hell's wrong with these people? I just fucked their daughter and spent the night in their home. I could be Ted Bundy for all they know.

I push the scrambled eggs around the plate with my fork and look up to see mom staring at me. She's hot, in that suburban mom/married woman/forbidden fruit/sexual tension kind of way. I smile at her. She smiles back and moves her hair with her hand so half her face is hidden in stiff strands of peroxide blonde.

"I gotta be getting back to Kansas City," I say to no one in particular.

"Missouri?" says the dad, and I get nervous all over again.

"Yeah, I guess? That's where the band is."

"What band?" asks the mom.

"Subhumans," I say, and wonder where the band is and if they're all right.

Patti looks at me and smiles. She's trouble, but I already knew that.

"Mom, I'm gonna go with Patrick."

"Okay, honey. Just be home for supper. Making your favorite, meatloaf."

"Yummy," says Patti.

I chug the rest of my beer, sneak another cigarette, and stand up. "Thanks for breakfast."

Dad nods, but he doesn't look at me. The mother smiles and stares off into space. The kid sneers and follows my every move. Patti grabs my hand and drags me back down the hall. Inside her room she jumps up kissing me, shoving her tongue down my throat. I'm a little surprised. I'm kind of freaked out. I'm getting hard and feeling none too good about it.

"I wanna go on tour," she says and grabs a backpack and starts shoving in clothes.

"Wait a minute. I can't take you with us. It's a small van. There's no room."

"You said I could last night."

"Did not," I say and wonder if I did.

We're in the van. It's in one piece. I thankfully didn't smash it up in a blackout last night. I'm heading north on Highway 35. Tall buildings are off in the distance, which I'm guessing is Kansas City. Although apparently there's two, one in Kansas and one in Missouri, which is confusing as hell. Around us the suburbs stretch for miles. It's all spread out and endless and I have no idea where the band is. Patti sits slumped in her seat. I didn't let her bring her backpack of clothes. She's pouting. I couldn't give a shit. I really just want to ditch her. But I'm feeling guilty, or responsible, or maybe I'm just off my game because I need to shoot some heroin. I've got a small last hit stashed in my bag but it's at the apartment with the band. If I can just get to the club then I can find my way back to the apartment and everything is going to be all right. I remember it was by the river. I think there was a bridge.

"Patti? How do I get to the club?"

"What club?"

"Last night, the club. The Foolkiller."

"Who cares?" she says. "The fucking place is closed."

"Just tell me where it is."

"Take this exit."

I drive down the offramp, there's train tracks, and plain brick warehouses. Nothing looks familiar.

"Pull over here."

I stop at the curb and Patti jerks open the door and jumps out. "Fuck you," she screams and slams the door.

I turn to watch as she runs down the street. It's a one-way. There's too much traffic and no way I can back up. I can't just leave the van in the middle of the street. She's gone and I don't know where the fuck I am.

***

I've been up for days and all I want to do is sleep. We're in Cleveland in a shithole club. I'm sitting at the bar. Drinking beer, waiting to get paid, and thinking about a bed in a nice motel. Hell, even a not-so-nice motel would do. A beautiful woman is sitting next to me. I glance her way and smile.

"Know who she is?" says the blonde next to her.

I look over at the blonde. She's rough all over, not just on the edges. I take the opportunity to give the beautiful woman a good stare and say, "No."

"She was on the cover of Roxy Music."

Okay, so like the beautiful woman is, well, beautiful. But what's a beautiful woman like her doing at a Subhumans' show, or worse, in Cleveland? And at the very least I can take it one step further and wonder how the fuck this beautiful woman who frequents dive bars and hangs out with rough-looking blondes could somehow manage to be on the cover of a Roxy Music album?

"You're gonna have to be more specific. Like was it pin-up girl in pink first album, or black satin blonde *For Your Pleasure*?"

"Neither," says the rough blonde. Then she pulls on her gum, making a long string, which she twirls around her finger before jamming it back in her mouth. I'm thinking she thinks this is sexy, but it's kind of more like, "Damn girl, what the fuck's wrong with you?"

"It was *Country Life*," she says, and points at the beautiful woman, I guess just in case I'm having trouble following the conversation, and with that distracting, weird gum move of hers she wasn't making it easy.

"Really? Black panties or white panties?"

"Black panties. Gonna buy us a drink?"

I'm trying to imagine the cover of *Country Life*. I mean, I know there are two hot looking women on the cover. I did, after all recall, the discrepancy in underwear. I'm thinking, *Girl in the white had a see-through bra. Girl in black covered her bare tits with her hands*. I remember staring at that girl's taught, tanned stomach for hours. That was 1975, I was eighteen years old, and there weren't a lot of half-naked women on album covers in those days.

"Love your work," I say lifting my glass to the beautiful woman sitting next to me.

She purses her lips and pulls out a cigarette.

"I'm drinkin' Seven and Sevens," says the rough blonde.

"You're not on a Roxy Music album cover," I say, then light the beautiful woman's cigarette.

"Yeah, but I'm with her, and she is."

There's no way I could say whether this woman is the woman on the cover. Even if she stood in front of some leafy bushes, got naked down to her lacy black panties, and covered her boobs with her hands, I still couldn't be sure. Although she is damn beautiful, the years just don't add up, and we're in Cleveland. Not exactly fashion model capital of the world.

"Need some sleep," I say.

"That's a strange pick-up line," whispers the beautiful woman.

She's got a husky, smoke-damaged voice with the hint of a German accent. I get a torque in my chest listening to her, which is either the speed wearing off or lust.

"No, seriously. Haven't slept in days."

"There's a bed at my place."

If I'm hearing right, she's offering me her bed. In my state of sleep-deprived delirium, she has got to be a hallucination from the meth/heroin combo platter that's been my life this last month. Then I feel her hand on my thigh.

"Uncle Pat!" Pete the Roadie shakes my shoulder. I turn towards him and stare for a few seconds, wondering who he is. It's not like Pete the Roadie is forgettable. He has a two-foot mohawk sticking straight up on his head. Only it feels like I've never really looked at him before. His skin's pasty white, he's got acne, he could use a shower. But all I can do is stare at his mouth as he speaks. There're bits of spittle flying everywhere, and his tongue is huge.

"Show's over, mate."

"Fuck, gotta get paid," I groan.

It takes every bit of energy I have just to get off the barstool.

"Don't leave," I say to the beautiful woman.

"Hey, where ya goin'?" yells the rough blonde. "Still got time before last call."

***

We're in Baltimore. I'm totally lost and don't know where the show is. I have been calling the promoter, but no one is answering. It's a total DIY show in a loft somewhere. So it's not even a venue anyone's ever heard of. I'm thinking a loft in a warehouse—a part of town where rent is cheap. But as I aimlessly drive through Baltimore everything looks like a goddamn warzone. Who the hell would pay rent to live anywhere in this fucking town?

I pull over to ask a skinny dude with messy hair wearing torn black Levi's, Converse sneakers, and a leather jacket if he's ever heard of the place. He shakes his head, wants to know if I have a spare cigarette, and then stands there. He's shaking all over and I realize he's not a punk, just a skinny-ass crackhead in a leather jacket he probably stole and little to no hygiene habits.

"Fuck."

"What you mean ya don't know where the venue's at?" says Dick.

"I'm hungry," says Pete the Roadie.

Pete the Roadie is always hungry, or thirsty for beer, or in need of a cigarette, or... fuck. You name it.

I fucking hate DIY shows. I like itineraries. I like real venues. I like load-ins and sound checks. I like promoters with telephone numbers and clubs that have listings in phonebooks.

The crackhead is still standing by the van, fidgeting. I'm fishing out a cigarette for him when I look over his shoulder at a telephone pole with flyers taped all over it.

"Shit," I say, momentarily forgetting the crackhead's smoke. I walk over and take a look. There's a shitload of flyers for different shows. I lift off the top one and there's a Subhumans poster underneath it. There's even an address. I carefully peel the flyer off and turn around to tell the band we're good. The crackhead is standing right behind me. Must have followed me over. He's got his hand out, waiting for the cigarette. But it disturbs me he's that close.

"Jesus Christ, dude. Back the fuck off."

And now he's got little sad crackhead eyes. Pleading for a smoke, his hand in his jacket pocket, probably fingering a knife. Dude would probably stab me for a nickel, let alone a pack of Camels.

"Here." I hand him a cigarette.

He takes it and just stands there with it pointing toward me.

Dude wants a light.

"What kind of dope fiend doesn't have a lighter?"

He shrugs and I light his cigarette. The crackhead looks happy as he exhales smoke through a crooked smile of crusty, chapped lips.

"What do we do now?" says Pete the Roadie.

"We go to the show," I say showing him the flyer.

The crackhead smiles and waves as we drive off.

The show is in a warehouse loft. With a flight of stairs going straight up to the top floor, for once I'm happy we don't have any gear. In the middle of this huge room there's a small stage with a drum kit and amps—better gear than we're used to borrowing. There's a bunch of underage kids milling around. I ask if they know where the promoter is. But apparently no one knows shit. Only it's still early, doors haven't even opened, so I'm not really worried.

There's no backstage, I really didn't think there was going to be. There is beer though, plenty of it, and the other musicians are cool and we're all hanging out. Somewhere around my fifth beer I realize I haven't eaten anything all day but shrug it off and open another one.

The first band's setting up two huge fog machines and I'm thinking, *Really? In a small space like this?* Then they turn them on and chemical fog starts billowing out. Soon the room is entirely engulfed. I can barely see the person next to me.

A droning dirge-wall-of-noise erupts from the shrouded stage. It's loud as fuck. The bass and kick drum's vibrations hit me somewhere midlevel in the chest. The guitars are screaming banshees; in seconds my ears are ringing. Band members emerge from the fog, then slip back inside, disappear.

There's a young kid standing next to me. I tap his shoulder.

"Who is this?" I scream.

"FOG! Fear of God." he yells.

I stand there in awe. Their whole scene is incredible. Their music dark and intense.

The young kid leans into my ear.

"I'm the promoter," he says.

He looks twelve years old.

***

I've never been to The Channel. Actually, having worked mainly for the Kennedys I haven't done that many shows in Boston. The name Dead Kennedys just doesn't go over well here. But I have done my fair share of shows in New Jersey, New York, Chicago, and Philly so I'm not unfamiliar with dealing with "reputed mobsters" in the music industry. Yet, the lumpy guy who runs The Channel is like a caricature, your stereotypical Italian thug: gold chains and velour tracksuit.

We're backstage drinking beers, waiting to go on. It's an all-ages show, and it's early. But with Jerry's Kids, D.Y.S., and Kilslug on the bill there's a good crowd. We've no merch, which seems to upset the lumpy guy. Like maybe we're not a real band if we don't have T-shirts. Plus, as with the rest of the tour, we're borrowing gear from the opening bands which makes him even more skeptical.

"Whatta you guys called again?" he says.

"Subhumans."

"You from England?"

"Yeah."

"Where's your accent?"

"I'm American."

He shakes his head and tells me to come to his office. I follow him and another guy who's huge, dressed in a black leather sport coat and fingerless gloves. In the office there are two other guys wearing pretty much the same uniform as the huge guy. They're smoking cigarettes, drinking beers, and laughing. They fall silent when we come in.

Lumpy guy sits down at his desk, pulls out an envelope, and tosses it towards me. I pick it up. There's money in it, not a lot, quick glance tells me about half our guarantee.

"This is light," I say.

Lumpy guy shrugs his shoulders, stares at me. I check my bearings, notice the huge guy is getting closer, the other two are now both standing, and everyone is staring at me.

"What can I say?" says lumpy guy. "You don't have a great draw."

"Where's the paperwork? What's the gross, the expenses? How you figure this is our take?"

"Looked at the crowd. Maybe you should too."

"You know what 'guarantee' means?"

"Know what 'can't sell out a show' means?"

"You agreed to the terms."

"Now I'm disagreein'."

"This is fuckin' bullshit."

"My thoughts exactly. Joey, show the sub'human gentleman out."

The huge guy steps next to me and herds me towards the door.

"Don't put your fuckin' hands on me. I want my money…"

The huge guy grabs the front of my leather jacket and shoves. Lumpy guy and his two cronies are laughing as the envelope of money lands at my feet on the greasy carpeted hallway floor.

The office door slams shut. I can hear them all yucking it up on the other side, or at least I think I can—the music on stage is of course too loud for me to hear anything. I pick up the cash that spilled out of the envelope and walk back into the club. The band is on stage. This is our last show. I'm fucking tired of promoters, shitty clubs, and driving. I need a drink and, hopefully, I score some heroin.

WE'RE A HAPPY FAMILY
1984: SAN FRANCISCO

There are several notorious "punk houses" in San Francisco: Fulton Street, A-Hole, The Fillmore House, The South Van Ness House, the House of Morons, the House of Lewd, and then there's Mission A. Located at 2450A Mission Street, right smack in the middle of the Mission District. An unmarked door off the entrance to Umberto's Tax Service leads upstairs to a former boarding house from back when the now predominately Latinx Mission was an Irish neighborhood. Still the same configuration with two connected floors holding five rooms each with a long, curved staircase between the two—the bottom floor speed freaks, the top floor heroin addicts—although no one would actually admit that was true.

As one can imagine, there's constant tension between the two factions. I try to keep a low profile but that isn't always easy. Anna Lisa and I middleman a lot of dope deals and our "customers" want to shoot up in the bathroom and sometimes that presents a problem. Shooting heroin is not an exact science. You do too much. You OD.

Anna Lisa never asked any of the roommates for permission for me to move in, and I still sort of pretend like I'm just visiting. I know everyone who lives there: D.H. Peligro (Dead Kennedys), Rachel Thoele (Mudwimin/Flipper), Chi Chi (Den mother to the Jaks), Steve DePace (Flipper), Robert "Sweet" Sweeting (Killer Wimps), and Michelle Rebel (bartender), and none of them have actually ever confronted me or even asked what I'm doing there. Except Sweet who is always giving me shit, but that's just him.

Anna Lisa's room is on the top floor, in the back, off the kitchen. Anna Lisa and I spend a lot of time together at night and weekends, but during the week Anna Lisa's out all day cutting hair for a living which leaves me alone with nothing to do except shoot drugs and wait around for another tour.

For the most part, I'm not a full-blown junkie. Or at least I like to think I'm not. In my mind, I'm more of a "recreational drug user with a slight habit." Not the monkey-on-my-back, two-hundred-dollars-a-day bank robbing drug habit it will eventually become.

I've been "chipping" like this for a while now. Never really thinking about it until I'm dope sick. Kicking still feels like a bad cold. In fact, the first time I thought I had the flu until an older junkie schooled me, "You're jonesing, man," and I realized I had a habit.

Most days I supplement my heroin intake with copious amounts of alcohol, various pills, the occasional snort of speed, or if I'm really in need, someone else's coke. (I never buy that shit—a totally unsatisfying drug.)

When I'm home, I'm in junkie mode. On the road, I taper off before the tour and then enjoy an occasional nod when the opportunity arises. Sometimes this arrangement goes awry and I can't control my using. Mostly, I keep it under control and the bands, for the most part, have no idea I'm an addict.

TRUST YOUR MECHANIC
1984: DEAD KENNEDYS

It's a bright, sunny day and being awake and already loading our gear onto a flatbed stage in a huge, vacant dirt lot on Mission Street is a little strange. Not strange that Dead Kennedys are playing for Rock Against Reagan outside the Democratic Convention, but strange that I'm home in San Francisco and already out of bed before the sun has gone down.

The RAR stage is in the "protest zone" outside the Moscone Center. MDC, The Dicks, DRI, Reagan Youth, and Michelle Shocked are all on the bill. By 3 PM, it's already crowded with thousands of people swarming the area. There are several political factions with plans for protests and roving political actions throughout the financial district and downtown.

From the minute we get there, it's a chaotic mess. D.K.s have already played several RAR gigs, and we're well versed in how they run their shows. With no real backstage area, the RAR organizers have loosely barricaded a section for the bands and gear. By show time, I've smoked two packs of cigarettes and I'm totally covered in dust. Never one to actually prepare for the elements, I'm also sunburnt as hell. What's worse is we're in a vacant lot and there's nowhere to take a piss or shoot drugs. It's like my worst nightmare come true. I'm hoping the Kennedys' set will be short and we can get the fuck out of here.

Biafra is totally in his element. He's got his audience and the political backdrop of the convention. Hellbent on making a statement, he screams through, "Nazi Punks Fuck Off," and launches into his usual theatrics pantomiming a firing squad victim for "Holiday in Cambodia."

The band rips through their set. Dust rises up from the pit in front of the stage. People are everywhere—hanging off the side-fills, crowding around the gear—and there's no room to move. Normally, I'd be clearing the stage, but this show is different. There's a need to show solidarity. The politicians need to see and hear us. We're not going away anytime soon. This is the politics of music. We want to be loud and in your face.

***

Gary Tovar's Goldenvoice Olympic Auditorium shows are legendary. This one is being billed as an international event with Dead Kennedys, B.G.K., Raw Power, Riistetyt, Reagan Youth, and Solución Mortal. The Olympic is an old boxing arena on the edge of downtown Los Angeles. It's one of those huge cement buildings where the sound bounces around and echoes and can be a nightmare when there aren't enough people in the audience. The main room is immense and capable of seating ten thousand. Backstage there's a warren of passageways and dressing rooms. Load-in is easy as we drive the van inside and drop off the T-shirts and gear.

D.O.A.'s management from Canada, Ken Lester, and his girlfriend Kris Carleson, are now managing the Kennedys and both of them are on tour with us, traveling in an old school bus with their entourage of Canadians, a few of whom will be selling our T-shirts. Thankfully, Microwave and I will be driving separately in the van, keeping us more autonomous and on our own schedule.

Tovar's security is always over the top. He hires a ton of local punks to work stage as well as the uniformed security that work the Olympic. Knowing the Kennedys are going to attract the usual Nazis and contact sports lovers, Tovar has lined the front of the stage with large dudes, most of them actually sitting on the stage to prevent access from the audience.

Micro is at the soundboard. I'm working the stage. I know a bunch of Tovar's guys from previous shows and through T.S.O.L. They're all punks out of Orange County. The Kennedys don't use their own laminated backstage passes, so everyone's wearing a Goldenvoice adhesive cloth "all access" patch. It's hard to tell who's working and who's a guest just taking up space.

I'm hanging on the side of the stage and it's utter mayhem. The bouncers are tossing stagedivers and fucking people up. But at least the gear is not getting trashed.

A large jock forces his way through the line of bouncers. Up on stage he tackles Biafra and pins him down with a straight-up wrestler move—twisting Biafra's leg behind his back. Biafra cries out in pain and desperately looks around for help. I'm on the other side of the stage and can't get to him. There are too many people in the way. By the time security gets their hands on the guy, the damage has been done and Biafra is hurt. He limps the rest of the show but doesn't stop singing.

Later that night, Carleson takes him to the ER and the diagnosis is severe sprained muscles and torn ligaments. The doctors put Biafra in a large and cumbersome Velcro leg cast that he'll have to wear the entire tour. A sitting duck in the middle of the stage, making him more of a target than usual for all the angry skinheads and jocks he verbally taunts and torments every night.

***

The sign says "Banning California, population 15,021." I'm thinking, *How long does the population stay the same so the sign is accurate? What happens when someone dies or simply moves away?*

Do they change the sign? Shouldn't there be those rotating numbers on wheels, like old-fashioned gas pumps, so the town government can keep it up to date?

I'm driving. Microwave is asleep. We're on our way to Phoenix. Last night, Micro showed up at our hotel room with two women from the show. I was tired and just wanted to sleep before we have to drive all day.

"They missed their ride," he says. "They live out in the desert, in Banning. Told 'em they could spend the night in our room. We'd get them home on our way to Phoenix."

Microwave already has his sights on one of the women which is okay by me as the other women is beautiful. She tells me her name's Michelle. We share my bed and sort of cuddle. I feel like I'm in high school, all of us in the same room making out. Well, that is if I ever actually went to a normal high school—which I didn't.

Michelle's hesitant or unsure—like she doesn't really want to have sex, or she's not that into me, or I don't know what. So I don't push it, and we mostly just talk, have fun, and laugh, while Microwave wrestles with the other woman in the bed next to ours.

Sometime around 4AM, I slip into the bathroom to shoot dope. I'm trying really hard to stay clean this tour, but I've a habit. I'm maintenance shooting the little heroin I've brought. The idea of kicking on the road scares me and I don't want to think about it.

"What were you doing in there?" asks Michelle.

"What do you mean?"

"You took so long."

"What are you, my mom?"

I light a cigarette and ignore her.

It's 10AM and we're all in front of the hotel. The band loading into the bus, and Microwave and I getting in the van. East Bay Ray puts the moves on the girls and offers them a ride. I look over and he's got this shit-eating grin on his face and I'm thinking,

Fucking band gets all the girls. But then she really wasn't into me, I've a girlfriend at home, and besides, I'm in love with heroin.

"It's better that way," says Micro. "We have to pick up the T-shirts in Long Beach."

The van feels unresponsive. It just doesn't have the power it usually does. I press on the gas and it hesitates, then revs, and there's a really loud banging coming from the undercarriage in the rear as if someone is beating a sledgehammer against the axle. There's no power and as I'm looking in the rearview mirror to change lanes there's an even louder noise. The driveshaft flies out the back of the van, narrowly missing the car behind us. Coasting, I pull onto the shoulder of the highway.

Asleep in the passenger seat, Microwave jolts awake. "What the fuck was that. What'd you hit?"

"Didn't hit shit."

There's white smoke billowing out of the hood as we get out on the passenger's side. It's burning hot in the sun. I'd had the windows down so it didn't feel that hot, but now that we've stopped it's unbearable.

"Fuckin' hell." Microwave has the hood up and we're both staring. The motor's been shoved through the radiator. The fan practically pushed through the front grill. A puddle of Day-Glo green antifreeze is forming on the ground. I get down on my knees and look under the van. Of course, there's no driveshaft and the U-joints are shorn off the deferential.

"I'll go call a tow truck. Stay with the van."

Across the highway are dull gray mountains. The desert stretches out for miles and everything shimmers like a mirage in the heat. Next to a gas station are two giant stucco dinosaurs. They've got to be at least forty feet high.

"That's fucking weird." I say out loud.

About a quarter mile down the road I see the driveshaft in the middle lane. When the traffic lets up, I run out and pick it up. It's lighter than I thought it would be and burning hot to the touch from being in the sun.

Micro's sitting in the van when I get back. "We're fucked," he says.

An hour later, the tow truck arrives and takes us to a repair shop. We talk with the mechanic. The van's not going anywhere. The tow truck driver, a nice guy chewing tobacco, gives us a lift to a motel.

We've got the band's gear and the merchandise, and we're definitely missing tonight's show. When we finally get a phone call through to Ken Lester, we make plans for Gary, the bus driver, to head back to Banning and pick us up. With no van, everyone will be traveling in the school bus for this tour.

***

We're at a motel in Phoenix. Microwave and I drove all night with Gary to catch up with the tour. It's late afternoon and we've a few days off and we're not in a hurry. We take a swim in the motel pool and hang out. The Kennedys' gear and T-shirts are packed in the back of the bus under a platform bed.

Later in the day when we all start loading into the bus, I realize it's already full of Canadians. Nancy "Chuck" Humphries, Allison and Leslie Jambor, and Candace Batycki all signed on to sell the Kennedys' merchandise. Gary Taylor is the driver. Ken Lester and Kris Carleson are a combo of management and road manager. Luxury Bob is a roadie, (although no one told me he'd be working with us), and Ron Shasberg and his girlfriend Lisette are visiting from Holland and along for the ride.

Microwave and I try to find our place on the bus. Everyone's welcoming but it's crowded and a little weird to be touring with such a huge crew. I'm used to it just being me and Micro in the van, and maybe Chris or Tracy too. Once in a while one of the band members catches a ride, but really it's a lot of night drives with solitude. Zen meditating. Zoning out on the empty highway.

We're all smoking cigarettes and drinking beers, which is one advantage of being on the bus. Micro, always in charge and not wanting to get busted, doesn't allow alcohol in the van while driving. Our next gig is El Paso. Then we've a long thousand-mile drive across Texas to a gig in Houston. I fucking hate driving across Texas. For once, I'm happy I'm not behind the wheel.

***

There are five other bands on the bill: B.G.K., Offenders, Cause For Alarm, and Orgasm. The venue is the Consolidated Arts Warehouse, scenically located in the industrial section of Houston, Texas, under an elevated highway. The promoter is an unknown and the band has never used them or played the venue. Although, theoretically it should be a good gig as surprisingly Houston has a decent music scene.

Unfortunately, even before the doors open there are problems, and it's immediately apparent things are out of control and perhaps too ambitious for the promoters—who we later find out are inexperienced and overwhelmed. It's an all-ages show with very little security. There's no alcohol being sold, yet everyone's drunk or whacked on drugs. The sound system isn't the best, but it'll have to work—four bands are going to beat the shit out of it before we even get on stage.

Gangs of skinheads are running commando raids into the crowd, making the pit a free-for-all slam fest. The backstage is crowded chaos. I spend most of my time watching the gear and making sure the zealous fans stay out of the dressing rooms and leave the band alone. Outside the temperature is in the hundreds.

Inside, with all the thrashing bodies and no air conditioning, it's probably 120 degrees.

All the Kennedys are in the building and the gear is set up. The Canadian's are selling T-shirts. It should be an easy show, but I'm hurting. Although I've been able to score a good amount of heroin, enough to last until we get to New Orleans, I'm not doing well physically.

Two days ago, in El Paso, I went out to dinner with my friend, George Packham, and his wife, Ali. On the way back to my motel, a drunk GI, AWOL from the local army base, ran a red light and plowed his Ford Torino into George's Toyota. The impact had sent us spinning through the intersection, up on two wheels, the driver's side of the car completely crushed. George's head had slammed into the doorframe and was bleeding. I didn't think I was hurt until I got out of the wreck, stood up, and realized I'd tweaked out my neck and back. The serviceman, so fucking wasted he had no idea what happened, kept trying to start his car. He'd rammed us so hard the front was crushed. He wasn't going anywhere—except off to jail and then probably into the army brig.

Tonight, my entire body is in agony. I can barely turn my head. But it's not like I can take a night off and sit in the tour bus and heal. I shoot just enough dope to ease the pain, not be in a nod, and keep on going. Thankfully, Ron and Luxury Bob help load the gear.

By 10PM I've yet to meet anyone who says they're in charge. I had to get the band's beer from an underage kid who said he was the stage manager. The sound guy is whacked, like he's smoking angel dust. The entire warehouse is this eerie, dark, cavernous space. The backstage area dimly lit. Young kids are wandering everywhere. It's anarchy and fucking out of control.

It's 11PM and the other bands have played. It's time for the Kennedys. I'm backstage getting the band together. "It's fuckin crazy out there, Slick," says Microwave before he heads off to the soundboard. "It's just you against the world."

"Thanks." I'm walking in front of the band, leading them to the stage. I've got my shirt off and I'm covered in sweat. I walk out and the crowd starts screaming and applauding, thinking I'm Biafra—just another pale white guy without a shirt. I look back and Biafra has stopped, the band is behind him, and he won't come out. He's pissed off and waiting for the applause to die down so he can make his own entrance.

The crowd is jacked up, drunk, sweaty, pressing against the stage, screaming, and wanting more. In the middle of the room groups of skinheads are waiting, poised for the chaos before the storm. I feel a gob on my back, as some asshole spits on me. I look around, but all I get are glaring eyes, and expressions of anger— adolescent angst and testosterone.

When the band finally comes out, the place erupts. The minute they start playing, cans and bottles and shoes start flying through the air. The pit immediately forms, and a shit load of punks start jumping on and off the stage. Whatever front of house security there was is long gone. I'm knee deep in stagedivers trying to keep them off the gear, away from the amps, and D.H.'s drum kit. The constant onslaught of bodies is brutal.

Biafra is mid-stage, clutching the mic stand. He's wearing his Velcro leg cast and is not as agile as usual. This makes him more of a target and I'm running interference. Luxury Bob is on the other side of the stage tossing people off and keeping it clear. Ron is there with him, but I don't know him or if he can take care of himself. I tell him to be safe and stay back out of the way. The last thing I need is one of us getting hurt.

A group of skinheads assault the stage en masse, trying to knock over the gear and fuck with Biafra. The second time they pass through I grab one in a chokehold and send him flying backwards into the audience. Which is me throwing down the gauntlet, now it's on, and they've got a new focal point to fuck with.

Another one dives into the drum kit. I pick him up by his back collar and belt, shuffle him headfirst off the stage, and then right the cymbal stands and start picking up the floor toms. With Ron's help, I get D.H.'s kit somewhat back together. The band keeps playing.

I turn around as two skins charge across the stage. I duck out of the way of the first dude and get clocked in the head by the second. I fall down to one knee. The other skinhead grabs Biafra's empty mic stand and swings, hitting me hard in ribs. I hear them crack on impact. Only it's so fucking loud on stage, that's impossible. The wind knocked out of me, I'm gasping for air, trying to catch my breath. D.H. is gesturing to his cymbals. Half of them are knocked over. The crash is leaning on his knee, and he can't get it off. I grab the cymbals and then straighten his kick. Ron starts frantically gesturing. The skinhead who cracked my ribs is running full bore, with his head down, straight at me across the stage. I pick up the mic stand, and he starts to back pedal, trying to stop his forward momentum. I swing the stand and the round steel base connects with his head. He flips backwards, twirling up over the crowd and down onto the pit. The mosh pit opens and there's a cleared circle around him lying on the floor.

Biafra, totally unaware, doesn't stop singing and the band continues to play. I collapse the three-piece mic stand into one shaft and spin the base off so I have a solid steel club. I cross the stage and dive into the crowd. Skinheads are everywhere, on the peripheral of the circle, behind me, pissed off, glaring, and angry.

The dude on the floor is going into convulsions. He's shaking, doing spazzy fish movements, with his eyes rolled up in his head. Two of his skinhead buddies pull him up off the floor.

I meet eyes with the other skins. I'm holding the mic stand like a baseball bat. My face is dirty from hitting the stage floor. Ron emerges through the crowd behind me. I'm grateful for the unexpected backup. There's a gang of these fuckers and I don't want to fight all of them. If I don't do something now this is going to go on all night. Sooner or later I'm going to get nailed. There's only one of me and a shit ton of them.

It's you against the world.

None of the other skinheads want to fight. I help Ron on stage and head over to my usual place by Klaus. I reach down to grab a beer I've stashed behind the amp. A shooting pain rips through my side. I can barely breathe.

Biafra is frantically gesturing for his mic stand. It's still in pieces, the steel shaft at my feet, and I've no idea where the base is. Biafra is getting pissed. He wants to do his pantomime theatrics and needs the stand. I search the side of the stage until I find one of those tripod stands. The kind heavy metal dudes love. When I hand it over, his bewildered expression says I'm fucking nuts handing him this stupid stand. But he realizes if this is the stand I'm giving him, then that's all I have.

Biafra's covered in sweat, putting all his weight on his good leg. He's wearing green surgical gloves and this cool Sandinista T-shirt I've been bugging him to give me. Rivers of sweat pour out the gloves, and the T-shirt is ripped and soaked. Biafra is talking shit to the crowd. They're fucking eating it up.

I walk back behind the amps and kneel down. While Biafra's talking there won't be any stagedivers and I can rest. D.H.'s floor tom is tilting to the left. I start to get up, but Luxury Bob is there, and he re-adjusts the leg. Ron is by Klaus' amp, right where I usually stand. I chill out for a second and try to breath. Ron stops a kid from knocking over Klaus's amp and effortlessly tosses him off the stage. I sit down and relax.

***

The sun is rising behind us as the bus drives west. The elevated highway glides us above the bayous and swamplands. The cypress trees covered in Spanish moss are tinged with pastel hues as the glowing morning sunlight glistens on the murky water. It'd be a beautiful view if my ribs weren't killing me. I can hardly breathe. I've a cough and there's so much crud in my lungs they rattle when I exhale. I'm out of drugs and starting to feel the cold fingers of withdrawal. I ask Gary to pull over at the next stop with a decent store or at least a minimart.

I'm walking the aisles of a Circle K, seeing nothing that's going to help with the pain. In the medication section there's aspirin, Tylenol, cough syrup, ibuprofen, and Alka-Seltzer. For a quick second I consider downing a bottle of Nyquil. A few late nights at home when I'd been stuck without any drugs or alcohol has caused me to hit the all-night corner store only to discover it was past 2AM. There was no liquor for sale and my only alternative was Nyquil. Memories of puking green slime flood my mind and—not wanting to repeat any of that—I quickly recoil.

Behind the cash register is where they keep all the hard liquor and I scan the possibilities. Southern Comfort, generic gin, Ten High, Old Forester, peppermint schnapps, Smirnoff vodka, and even the old standby Dewar's White Label. But even the thought of cheap scotch doesn't appeal, and I go the absolute lowbrow route and get a big bottle of Mad Dog 20/20, orange Gatorade, and a bottle of ibuprofen. The kid at the counter doesn't even flinch and graciously gives me a plastic "to-go" cup. Perhaps this is the breakfast beverage of choice in Louisiana?

Sitting on the bench seat of the bus, I sip Gatorade laced with MD20/20 as the swamplands roll by. Ron gets up and sits in the seat next to me. We talk about Europe. He asks how I'm doing, says if I need any help on stage, he's there for me.

"Dude, you saw how it is. Kinda sketchy up there sometimes."

Ron tells me he's a kick boxer. "I'm not afraid of shit."

I'm holding my ribs thinking, *I am. I am afraid of getting stomped to death. I don't want to be cut again like in Denver. I'm afraid of running out of drugs. I'm full of fear and you should be too.* Instead of saying all that I just nod, "If you want, you can help. But don't cry to me if you get your ass kicked."

"Got your back Mickey. No one can kick my ass."

Ron calls me Mickey because when he asked what nationality I was I told him I was a mick, meaning Irish. He'd never heard that term, thought it hilarious. Now, I'm Mickey.

"Maybe when ribs heal, you stop doing all those drugs."

I like to think that no one knows I'm a junkie. Other than "partying" with the road crew, which really means drinking a shitload of beer and, if available, hard liquor, I don't score dope or get loaded with anyone else on the road. I sure as hell don't want the band knowing, and from what I gather, the rest of these folks are just casual users. I'm not seeing any track marks or pinned eyes. I don't know any of them well enough to divulge the extent of my drug habit.

"Maybe you mind your own business and shut the fuck up."

In 2017, I'll post a photo online that was taken in the '80s. I'm half nodded out and it's obvious I was loaded on heroin. I'll caption the photo with: "Back when drugs were working." I do this as a joke. Ron will take offense and send me a message, "You know I always liked you, but when you were on drugs, I hated you! 1985 hotel room, I found you laying on a bed, out! Lisa and Chris smiling their life away, I pounded you so hard on your chest you were black and blue the next day, but I got you back! 1986 Mission Street S.F., I found you half dead in your bed with Lisa, dragged you out and threw you on a couch. I believe it was in the hallway (I think Rebecca was with me), called an ambulance, and they put the big needle in you, whoops Patrick was awake again! Brother, I loved you back then just like I did Chris, but hell did you guys make it difficult for me sometimes. How cool would it be though to meet each other one day??? Love Ron. I am glad you have the life you have right now, wish Chris was still here!"

I get off the bus in New Orleans and it's like walking into a big, hot, sticky, wet blanket smothering me so hard I can barely breathe. The club is on the other side of town from the French Quarter. It's sort of desolate and all the streets are named for trees. Across the road there's a huge barn for the streetcars. A workman, shrouded in a spray of sparks, is using a grinder on one of the car's bumpers. There's simplicity to what he's doing. I almost envy him for his regular Joe day job, but then maybe it's just that I scored some good powdered brown heroin from a street dealer outside the motel and I'm finally well again.

The Butthole Surfers are on the bill tonight. It'll be good to see familiar faces. Microwave and I start unloading gear. Luxury Bob is nowhere around. Ron stayed back at the motel. This is the problem with "visiting" roadies. They want to do the stage work where everyone sees you and it's fun to be part of the show. The real job, the not-so-glamorous humping gear part, nobody really wants to do.

It's so fucking hot I'm drenched in sweat. My clothes are thoroughly soaked. Microwave has his shirt off. He's cut and muscular. I'm not. I'm ashamed of my belly, un-muscular chest, and skinny arms. I keep my ripped T-shirt on and suffer the heat.

Twenty years later, a photo of me naked to the waist at a Dead Kennedys show in Reno, circa 1984, will surface on social media. I stare at it now and think, What the hell was I worried about? *I look okay. I'm not cut with ferocious abs by any means. But I'm not the overweight guy I felt I was then either. In fact, I just sort of look normal. Like most people who have gotten older, I'm almost*

*envious of how I looked. A woman I know comments saying I'm
"manorexia" and it hits me again how much I stressed about shit
that didn't matter.*

It's sunshine, mayhem, controlled anarchy, and once again
time to play outdoors for another Rock Against Reagan show, only
this time in front of the National Republican Convention in Dallas,
Texas. Cause For Alarm, Reagan Youth, and a reggae band are also
on the bill. Our school bus is parked alongside a few other buses by
the temporary stage in the back of a chain-link fenced-in section of a
park—a good ways off from the Dallas Memorial Convention Center.
Unlike the Democratic Convention in S.F., we're boxed in and well
contained. On either side of us are similar areas reserved for other
protesting factions, known as "free speech zones," and as the day
progresses, we learn that one of the protesting factions will be the
daughters and sons of the Christian organization The Concerned
Christians for Reagan, as well as members of another Christian
group, Young Americans for Freedom; and the word is that they will
be here protesting against us.

As Reagan Youth's lead singer, Dave Insurgent, prowls the
stage growling lyrics, a mass of Christians floods the adjoining free
speech zone. Soon their voices are added to the excess barrage of
noise. Dressed in a loose uniform of khaki slacks and pleated skirts,
button down white shirts, ties, and penny loafers, the Christian
youths scream obscenities at us through the fence. Many are holding
signs that read "Family Values" and shout, "We're Christians for
Reagan!" The ones closest to the fence shout, "Fuck you!"

On the other side, a group of Iranians arrive en mass
supposedly protesting for pro-monarchy in Iran and are rabidly anti-
Khomeini. With fists raised they yell, "Death to Khomeini! Death to
Khomeini!" Just like the young Christians, the crowd is women and
men. But unlike their Christian counterpart, there's a decidedly
staged affect to the Iranians' protest. I'm not feeling their outrage,

it's as if they're just going through the motions and, in the end, they too seem to be directing their anger towards us.

By the time the Kennedys are scheduled to play, it's total chaos. Outside the fenced-in area several squads of cops in riot gear and carrying truncheons have assembled—waiting for a reason to start breaking heads. Inside the fence, we're so pushed up together that along the backstage the Christian youths pressed against the fence try to grab us as we pass by. An enraged blonde girl dressed in tennis whites snarls, "Y'all goin' to hell!" as a bottle of water flies through the air above my head. On the other side, a young Iranian couple stands by the fence and stare at me with hate and it's weirdly awkward. The woman's brilliant blue eyes dig into my soul and her beauty momentarily stops me until she screams, "Death to infidels!" The man at her side shakes his fist and spits at me.

On stage, Biafra takes the mic and the band rips into "Kill the Poor" and "Moral Majority." A small pit opens up and a few even slam dance. But the surrounding cops intimidate the crowd and most of them just stand around waiting to see what will happen. In the distance a group of conventioneers leaves the building as the Republicans take a dinner break. Biafra screams over the PA, "They're leaving the convention!" and gets the crowd to start chanting, "Fuck off and die!"

Ron and Luxury Bob are both up on stage and, after Houston, I'm stoked to have back up. A small gang of jocks who look similarly like the young Christians are wandering through the crowd, shoving people trying to start something, but are mainly ignored. Somewhere in all this, an American flag is burned and a battalion of cops move in, pushing through the crowd and make a big show of arresting the guy who torched the flag.

Eventually, the Christian youths get tired and leave. The Iranians disappear. The band finishes the set and the cops swarm the area, forcing the audience to move away. In less than twenty minutes, it's an empty field covered in trash, and we hurry to pack up the gear.

SUICIDE CHILD
1984: SAN FRANCISCO

We're in our loft dope sick trying to kick heroin one more time. Anna Lisa is in bed next to me, unconscious on somas and Valiums, thrashing around in a fitful imitation of sleep. We did our last hit two days ago. Today, we've taken nothing but pills. My skin is crawling off my body. All my muscles are spastically twitching. I'm drinking a large bottle of red wine. Every twenty minutes I run to the bathroom and throw up. I've puked so much there's nothing left in my stomach. I taste bile. Covered in sweat, I'm oddly very loaded, but the agony of withdrawal bleeds through and I feel every moment of pain. All I can think about is shooting dope to make it all go away.

"Fuck this shit." I swing my legs over the edge of the loft and feel around with my bare foot for the steps.

"What… are you doing?" Anna Lisa groggily reaches for me.

"Can't take it." I push her hand away.

"Just lay back down."

"I'm going up the street."

Four blocks away on Mission Street is the dope spot and there's always someone out there slinging drugs. Although the later into night, the worse the drugs get and more the possibility of getting burned.

"I thought we were going to kick."

"Fuck that noise." I lunge for the stairs and slip. I try to regain my balance and fall down the stairs. I hit the floor, hard, jump up, and launch myself halfway through a window that overlooks the stairwell. In shock, I stand there naked and immobile, my knee stuck in the broken windowpane, held in place by a huge shard of glass stabbed into my skin.

"Fuckin' hell." I pull my leg back inside. The rest of the window falls and crashes on the roof below. I clutch my knee and pull out a huge piece of glass. Blood spurts across the room onto the white wall.

"Oh my fucking god." Anna Lisa grabs a towel and presses it against my wound.

"I'm going back to bed."

I put up a good front. Or at least I think I do. But if I'm not loaded, I'm in fear. I'm convinced the world knows I'm a fraud. I don't know what I'm doing. I have no clue how to live life, be successful, or find happiness. My whole identity is working in music and I'm only too sure the bands I work for are going to suddenly decide they don't need me. I can run away from everything when I'm on tour. I have low self-esteem, a big ego, and I want people to love me. Not just like me. But LOVE me. Yet I don't know how to love them back. Every time I stick a needle in my arm all that goes away. Only being strung-out with no money is taking its toll. I want to be loaded. I just don't want to deal with the consequences. And I don't want any of the bands to know I'm a junkie.

The ER nurse stares at me skeptically. "What are you on?"

I'm totally confused and disoriented. Kicking heroin makes you crazy. Kicking heroin, getting loaded on a ton of pills, drinking a bottle of red wine, and really hurting yourself makes you insane.

"It was self-inflicted." I'm not really sure why I say that. Perhaps I'm thinking the authorities believe Anna Lisa attacked me.

Really, I'm hoping this nurse will just go away, the doctor will appear, and someone will put me out of my misery.

"What was?"

"I fell."

"Onto a knife?"

The intern injects a local right into the wound. I watch as the needle probes the sliced flesh and I'm amazed I can't feel it. Then he calmly scrubs the cut with a brush and a yellowish disinfectant. The blood is still flowing everywhere and for the first time I wonder if I severed a main artery.

"How are you doing?" The intern looks up at me as he pulls the black thread through my skin, closing the wound.

"Can I go now?"

Two large orderlies are on either side of me as I hobble along, a pair of crutches under my arms. They're escorting me to the psych ward.

I just want to go home and shoot some dope.

WINNEBAGO WARRIOR
1984: DEAD KENNEDYS

It's my birthday. I'm twenty-eight years old. We're in Portland, Oregon. It's a cold night in October, winter is right around the corner, and I'm totally strung-out. I'd tried to kick before we left. But it didn't happen.

Until now, I've been able to keep it under control with some maintenance using for at least the first week or two of tour and then chip away on what I could score on the road. This time it's different and the jones is bad. I've already gone through what meager amount of drugs I could scrape together before we left. I'm dope sick and I don't know anyone I can score from in Portland. It's not like the shit isn't here. The Great White North is awash in smack—something about all that rain, dark gray skies, and cold weather makes being a junkie seem like the thing to do. Probably the same reason there's a huge suicide rate as well. You'd think an economically depressed shithole like Portland would be the perfect place to score. Only we're in some desolate neighborhood downtown and the weather is so bad the streets are deserted. Not even a helpful hooker out on a street corner to point me in the right direction.

I finally cop a dozen Valiums from a girl who works for the venue. I take three and wait for the calming effect, hoping I don't have violent withdrawals during the show. At least we're staying in a motel and not driving all night to the next gig. Thankfully, there's always beer backstage. I chug a shit-ton of Budweiser and hang out while the opening bands rip through their sets.

Typical of the Kennedys doing things the hard way, we're headed across Canada at the beginning of winter. Hell, we just did the South during the summer's sweltering heat. Why not Canada in the freezing snow?

I'm not really prepared for a Canadian winter. San Francisco may not be the warmest spot in California, but it's still California and I don't own a winter coat. I got a leather jacket, maybe a sweater, and a few cut-off T-shirts. I did bring a pair of gloves and I'm hoping to score a scarf before we cross the border.

When it's time to hit the stage, I take off my leather and stash it behind one of the couches in the dressing room. It's going to be hot on stage with the lights, and plus there's always beer getting tossed around. I really don't want my jacket soaked and smelling like a brewery. Normally, I stash it in the van. But it's too fucking cold to go back outside.

After the show, my leather jacket is gone.

Somebody ripped it off.

I'm fucking freezing.

I'm dope sick.

I'm pissed off.

***

Eugene, Oregon, might be just another small college town, but the audience is enthusiastic and the venue, the WOW Hall (Workers Of The World), is a weird hold over from the socialist WPA days of 1935 and is now a communal enterprise run by well-meaning hippies.

The opening band, Tales Of Terror, kicked ass. Hailing out of Sacramento, California they're a hardcore mayhem band fueled by copious amounts of alcohol and LSD. S.F. promoter Paul Rat is their manager and on tour with them. Over the years, I've had my run-ins with Paul, and I don't really like him. He can show an asshole side in a second flat, and I'm cautious around him and the guys in Tales Of Terror. But the lead singer, Rat's Ass, is cool and we hit it off immediately after it becomes apparent we know a lot of the same people. We're backstage laughing. He's so loaded I'm hoping he knows where to score some drugs. But he doesn't and I'm left to my own devices again.

The house crew dispenses the band's gear with utilitarian efficiency. We've never had so much help loading out. Micro and I have to practically physically stop them from putting the gear into the van.

"Thanks man, really. We got this."

There's a crowd of young college kids hanging around. Everyone is talking about the "after party." I'm keeping my eyes open for a nodding junkie, but there's a decidedly wholesome aura to all these kids, innocence on a weekend bender. Plus, they're all at least fifteen years younger than I am, college freshmen or even high schoolers.

"Dude, that was awesome."

A young kid holding a beer is standing next to me. He either materialized out of nowhere, or I'm losing my mind.

"What?"

"You dudes rocked."

"Um, yeah, okay."

"Going to the after party?"

"You know I've been meaning to ask someone, what's this after party?"

"The party after the show."

"Yeah, I got that part... but... "

"You work for the Dead Kennedys?"

"Looks that way."

Microwave says he's tired and going to the motel. I'm not drunk or the least bit loaded and not looking forward to a night of staring at the ceiling of my motel room unable to sleep. There has to be at least one opiate addict in this town. Someone with Vicodins or Dilaudids—hopefully the latter, as most Dilaudids are shoot-able.

"Dude, where's this after party?"

The kid tells me to come with him and he'll show me. When he tells his girlfriend I'm tagging along, she shoots daggers at me and says, "Whatever."

The kid is enthusiastically yammering on about his art collective, and I feel bad I'm so focused on scoring drugs that I'm not really paying attention. There was a time I cared about art. If I were already loaded, we'd be having a much different conversation. One I'd probably enjoy.

We're walking down a nearly deserted unlit street. It feels like we're out in the middle of the country. Only there's music and a lot of noise coming from a house a few blocks away. As we get closer, groups of kids are hurrying past us going the other direction.

"What's happening?" The kid asks.

"That band's tearing the place apart."

"What band?" Dead Kennedys are not a party-like-a-mad-dog-tear-up-the-house bunch of guys.

"They're on drugs!"

Dark silhouettes on the upper balcony of a two-story house shove a couch over the railing. Most of the windows are broken, there's glass all over the lawn. The front door is wide open. There are sirens in the distance getting closer, but I'm still contemplating going inside to look for drugs.

"Dude, you know where I can get any pain pills?"

The art collective kid looks confused.

"I hurt my back." I bend slightly forward trying to appear as if I'm hobbled over in pain.

"I've a friend that has Percocets."

***

I'm no longer dope sick. The kid's friend had a script of 60 mg pills. I bought the entire bottle, which is easily smuggled across the Canadian border under the battery in the engine compartment of the van.

Unfortunately, getting D.H. into Canada isn't as easy. The Canadians are holding up our entry citing D.H.'s past marijuana possession charge. The band and crew are sitting in a waiting room while the Mounties figure this shit out. The booking agency maintains his conviction had been acknowledged as part of the band's work permit and the correct bond had been posted. But the Canadian authorities are saying it wasn't. Or they just want to be assholes. After a long wait and several searches of our luggage, they let us through.

A few hours later we're in Vancouver, loading into the York Theatre for a two-night run. Although it's sort of sunny, it's still fucking freezing, and I'm again reminded I need to buy a jacket. All the Canadians are walking around in cut-off plaid shirts. I'm dressed in a T-shirt, a long sleeve shirt, and a raggedy sweater and I feel like a wuss for complaining about the cold. When Ray hands me money he collected from the band, I get as emotionally choked up as someone loaded on opiates can.

"You need a jacket," he says.

I head off to buy one before the show.

The Kennedys are hardcore, political, and in-your-face and Biafra is an acquired taste. People either totally love Dead Kennedys, or they absolutely despise them. There's no in between. Half the audience is there to hate them. The other half sings along with the lyrics and prop Biafra up when he jumps in the pit. Their music isn't the standard three-chord punk or breakneck fast. Their songs have melodies and rhythm and smart lyrics. They support leftwing politics, they're anti-fascists, they help other bands, and Biafra's Alternative Tentacles label puts out their records.

I was drawn to the D.K.s for all the above reasons. Working for them felt like the right thing to do. Dead Kennedys have the ability to influence a huge swath of kids that normally wouldn't have an alternative to America's rightwing agenda. Biafra's knowledge of local politics is astounding. He can banter with the best of them and knows his shit.

Vancouver is our kind of town, and this is our audience. The band is full on tonight. Ray's guitar work, while always on point, is superb. This tour he's been using a Carvin Telecaster played through an Echoplex tape delay, giving him his signature sound. Klaus's bass playing holds down the rhythm section and tonight he's a powerhouse, using his 1966 Lake Placid Blue Fender Jazz bass through a Traynor Monoblock with one overdrive pedal as an effect. Klaus is the supreme minimalist when it comes to gear.

D.H. is the best drummer I have ever seen. The man is on it from the minute he hits the stage. He can go from tight Gene Krupa jazz riffs to rapid-fire speed metal in two seconds flat. The sheer power he uses as he hits his drums is astounding. I have to keep my eye on them as they're slowly disintegrating from the abuse. He's been using the same Rogers kit for years and this tour they're starting to show their age. The tom legs are tightened with a drum key and the bolts' square heads and threading is wearing away. Two of them are problematic and the tom frequently falls forward as D.H. beats the shit out of them.

Then, of course, there's Biafra. His stage antics are legendary. His wardrobe occasionally bordering on absurd, he puts on more of a performance than the majority of lead singers. Due to his penchant of constantly stagediving into the audience, our contract rider requires promoters to lengthen his mic cords to fifty feet or more. Tonight on stage, backed by local roadie legend Chris Crud, I perfect my technique of trolling for Biafra. When he jumps into the audience, I grab the mic cord and let it out to its full length. With the audience holding Biafra aloft, I keep the cord above them, and when he makes his way back toward the stage, I reel him in.

All the Canadians from the summer tour are at the show at the side of the stage: Candace, Gary, Bob, Chuck, Kris, Ken Lester, and the guys from DOA. After the show, I hook up with Chuck and we go to a friend's house instead of the motel. I scored some China White at the club. When I spike it into my vein, a huge sense of relief washes over me. "I need more of this."

Chuck says she doesn't know anyone that's holding. I don't really believe her. But what choice do I have. I nod out all night and we have sex in between during bouts of consciousness. In the morning, I discover Chuck is not coming on tour. Somehow, I had thought she was and I'm disappointed.

San Francisco, 2006. I'm at an AA meeting in a church basement on Cathedral Hill. I've been clean and sober for just over five years, and I work as a drug and alcohol counselor at the rehab where I got clean. The meeting is over and, like usual, all the addicts and alcoholics are milling around, and the volume of voices is annoyingly loud. I'm standing in line to thank the speaker, a woman named Liz who's with Jimmy the Saint, another friend of mine in recovery. There's a woman in front of me talking to Liz. She's dressed in work clothes like Ben Davis or Dickies, complete with a regulation hat—as if she's in uniform. When she turns around, I realize it's Chuck. It's been almost twenty years since the last time we saw each other. Chuck looks different. I'm sure I do too. We start seeing each other. It lasts a few months. It doesn't work out. Sometimes you just can't return to the past.

The plan is the same as the summer tour. The band and Canadian crew will be in the school bus, and Micro and I will be in the van with the gear. A month ago, Microwave had picked up the van in Banning. The mechanic had totally rebuilt the driveshaft and differential mounts and replaced the radiator. Even with a hundred and fifty thousand miles on it, the van is still running strong.

We're on Highway 1 deep in the Canadian Rockies. I'm out of Percocets and feeling the first hint of withdrawal. We've stopped to get gas. I'm wearing my new leather jacket, but its twenty degrees outside, and I'm freezing. I've already walked the aisles of the convenience store, but nothing looks like it'll help my kick. This isn't a cracked rib, and MD 20/20 and Gatorade is not going to cut it.

At the next gas pump, there's a scruffy, overweight dude wearing a Black Flag T-shirt under his down jacket. I'm hoping he's some kind of drug addict or maybe he even knows where to score. I sidle up next to him and ask if he's holding. The dude squints his eyes and says no. From his response, I can tell he's never done drugs in his life and doesn't know what the hell I'm talking about. This is what it's come down to. I've totally lost my mind. I'm asking strangers where to score heroin. Desperate, I corner Candace before she gets on the bus. "I really need drugs."

"Don't we all," she says.

"I've a splitting headache. I'm dope sick."

"Aw, Patrick. Why you do this to yourself? Get a bottle of 222s and a can of high test. Ride it out."

"Two two whats?"

"222s. Codeine, caffeine and aspirin. Over the counter. Any drug store."

Across the road there's a Shoppers Drug Mart. I tell Micro I have a headache and I need aspirin, "I'll be right back." Fuck yeah, Canada, where you can buy codeine over the counter but need a prescription for antibiotic ointment.

There is something thoroughly disgusting going on inside of my body from ingesting copious amounts of these 222s. I want to puke, I want to take a shit, and I'm horribly constipated. Sadly, they don't get me high, but the jones is somewhat subsided, or maybe it's just the best placebo ever made. I'm pouring ten or more at a time into my mouth straight from the bottle and then chasing it with O'Keefe Extra Old Stock malt liquor which is probably not the worst thing I've ever done to stave off withdrawal. But it's close.

We've played Kamloops and Edmonton and we're on the way to Calgary. I'm on day three of withdrawal. I'm in no shape to drive and I'm faking I've a bad cold. Yesterday, I grabbed my bag out of the van and switched to riding the bus, leaving Micro to drive across Canada on his own. After a few days, it becomes apparent that I'm not fooling anyone with my "I've a cold" routine. Everyone knows I'm dope sick. Candace must have told Leslie and the rest of the Canadians.

There's a woman riding with us in the bus who works for the promoter. I figure if anyone knows where to get drugs in the prairie providences of Canada it's her. I pull out all the charm I can muster and flirt with her. She's nice but totally shoots me down. "I heard you were trying to kick." I'm guessing sniveling dope sick junky roadies aren't big on her wish list of sexual conquests.

Without drugs, it's mind-numbingly boring riding the bus. The flat plains of Canada roll by and there's absolutely nothing to look at. There's fucking snow everywhere. I fucking hate snow. I fucking hate winter. And I'm starting to fucking hate Canada.

***

We're on a four-lane highway, divided by a wide, wooded median that cuts through the dense forest of Wisconsin. We played Winnipeg two nights ago. It was our last Canadian show of the tour. The crew and promoter said their goodbyes, and I had to get off the bus and back in the van with Microwave and the gear. But the good news is I'm no longer dope sick (and thankfully out of 222s).

It's 2AM. I've been driving for over eight hours. Micro is in the back asleep. I'm kind of blurry eyed, but otherwise I'm on it. The highway is busy for this late at night. I'm passing trucks and 18-wheelers, making good time, headed for Chicago.

Another freezing winter night and the old van isn't anywhere near airtight. Cold wind seeps in through cracks, and the wing window is making a whistle that bugs the fuck out of me. I have the heater on full blast, barely making a dent in the freezing cold. I'm wearing two T-shirts, a sweater, my leather jacket, Levi's, boots, two pairs of socks, and gloves, which is about everything I own.

The road is slippery. Covered in ice. I'm careful not to make any sudden turns. I ease around a semi, pressing the pedal down, and gain some passing speed. Visibility is good. I'm hoping it stays that way. Although the gray, overcast sky looks like more snow is on the way.

There's a cold half-cup of coffee on the console. I stub out another cigarette into the overflowing ashtray and check the side view mirror for cops. The gas gauge is on a quarter tank. We'll need to stop soon.

I'm in the slow lane when a huge 18-wheeler comes barreling up, doing eighty-five MPH, matching my speed. We're dead-on, neck and neck, and I wonder what this guy knows that I don't. Last I checked, Wisconsin State Patrol weren't all that fond of truckers going balls-out on their highways. I could slow down. Let him pass. But what's the point? I'd still have to go around him again at the next incline.

We've both got our high beams on. Patches of ice shimmer in the headlights, and the road is slippery. An eighth of a mile in front of us, three deer rush into our lanes and prance, jittery and scared across the highway. I let up on the gas and so does the trucker. The deer clear his lane and he guns it. I hold my breath as they make their way towards the shoulder. I'm twenty feet away when the last deer stops and freezes in the headlights. She's almost off the road, just her ass is in the way, and I slowly press the brake pedal. I'm stuck in my lane. The truck has me hemmed in. I can't jam down on the brakes. That would send me into a tailspin across the ice-covered highway. It's all in slow motion. The deer turns her head. We make eye contact as the right front side of the van smashes into her hindquarters and spins her off into the darkness—the sound of the impact deafening.

A hundred yards and I've stopped on the side of the road. There's only one working headlight and I'm careful to make sure there's actually a shoulder to pull off on. I'm shaking. I feel sick to my stomach.

"What the fuck happened?" yells Micro.

"Hit a fuckin' deer." I've probably killed that beautiful living creature. She stared at me with human-like eyes, as if pleading for her life.

"Shit," says Micro. "We still drivable, right?"

The front passenger side of the van is crushed. The headlight's busted and hanging out of its frame like a gouged-out eyeball. There's blood and bits of fur caught in the chrome trim, grill, and bumper.

"Maybe I should walk back, makes sure she's…"

"What are you going to do if it's still alive?" says Micro. "Be all Daniel Boone, put it out of its misery with your Bowie knife?"

Microwave's right. I don't know what the fuck to do. I just keep playing the moment of impact over and over in my head. Her eyes, staring into mine, the sound when I hit her.

"Get in the van, Slick," says Micro. "I'll drive."

The truck stop's parking lot is an open asphalt field on a hilltop. The wind whips across it and through my clothes as I work the bloody bent bits of metal back to somewhat the same position they were before I hit the deer. Micro's in the restaurant getting coffee. We've filled the van with gas. The only real damage is the headlight, and some of the grill is gone. Another foot over and she would have taken out the radiator. I shove the busted headlight into the opening, but I can't get it back into its frame. It's too bent, and I can't just leave it hanging there either.

"Let me get the toolbox." Micro hands me a cup of coffee. It's hot and sweet with too much sugar. Fucking Micro's from Boston. They drink their coffee like this. They call it "regular" and unless you say otherwise, that's how you get it.

We're pulling road cases out the back of the van and stacking them outside on the ground. It's amazing how much shit we pack in this tiny space. Halfway in, a permeating stench fills the air.

"The fuck is that smell? Something die?"

"What the fuck you think it is?" Micro opens a road case and pulls out Biafra's parka.

Biafra drinks a concoction of cayenne pepper, garlic, and orange juice before every show. He claims it helps his voice. Opens up the old windpipes. Perks the vibrato. Afterwards, in the dressing room, Biafra drenched in cayenne garlic citrus sweat, he wants his parka. A full-blown hypochondriac, Biafra is prone to colds. The parka is his protection. It's like a talisman, part of the ritual, and we've been dragging the same stinky, sweat-soaked coat around for years. Summer tours, the back of the van reeks. Winter, it's more confined to the four-foot radius of the road case we carry just for storing it.

"That's gettin' really ripe." I'm waving off the fumes with one hand and sip coffee from the other.

"Fuck this." Micro tosses the coat on the ground. As he digs around looking for the toolbox, I pick up the parka and throw it in a nearby trashcan.

"Tell 'em some fan stole it. He'll believe that."

"Good thing you're wearing gloves."

***

It's a sold-out show in Green Bay, Wisconsin. The promoter has let in way more than is legal capacity and the room is packed. The only place that isn't crowded is the stage. The house crew and I are standing around after the opening band has done its damage and gotten off. Microwave, at the mixing board, jams Run-DMC into the house cassette player. The striped-down, heavy-breathing beat of "Hard Times" pumps though the stacks of the PA. Run-DMC's debut album had just been released and it's playing everywhere. Micro decided it's the official "before the Kennedy's go on" music. Plus it not only pisses off the punks, but Biafra hates it too. A few shows ago he screamed at Micro asking why the fuck it was always playing before he went on.

"It's the official opening music for this tour, that's why," said Micro.

Biafra didn't have a response. I'm sure he was wondering who had made it the official opening music. Did the rest of the band vote? Would he look like a jerk saying it wasn't? Instead of pulling rank and demanding we played some horrible crap no one's ever heard of, he just walked away sulking.

But for the road crew, it was a much-needed reprieve from having to listen to punk 24/7, and when we heard it, we knew we had exactly thirty-nine minutes before the band hit the stage.

I'm repositioning D.H.'s drums, which I know is futile, as every time I think I've got his setup down he'll rearrange it differently. Push the floor tom to the left, adjust the ride, push the kick farther away or closer to him. It fucking drives me crazy. When the house soundman starts mic'ing the kit, I tell him we'll have to re-do it once Darren starts playing. He looks at me as if I'm a moron and this is my first show. I say, "He repositions everything." Sound guy just shrugs. I know I'm on my own here.

Leaning against a side-fill looking out at the front of house I take a second before the mayhem starts. Drinking a beer, I bop my head, digging on the music.

"It's like that, and that's the way it is..."

There's a kid, twenty feet out in the audience, and he's staring at me. When our eyes meet, he shakes his head. I look at him and mouth "what?" Pointing toward the PA, he scowls and shakes his head again. Apparently, he doesn't like the music.

"It's fuckin' Run-DMC," I yell.

The kid flips me off.

After the show in the dressing room drenched in sweat, Biafra loses his shit over the missing parka. "I'm going to be sick!" he screams. "There goes the goddamn tour!"

After throwing his stuff around the room, he bundles up in whatever clothes he has and angrily paces the floor. I make myself scarce and stay clear of his verbal onslaught. Microwave, being the good road manager that he is, takes the brunt of the abuse. Later, the stage manager finds a musty old blanket and gives it to Biafra who wraps it around himself before leaving the club.

***

Lawrence, Kansas. It's a small hall, sold out, and filled to capacity. I'm tossing stage divers with one hand, while trying to keep the mic stands upright, gear intact, and the cables untangled. A fat-assed skinhead skips across the stage and leaps, Klaus's mic cable snagged around his foot. I dive into the crowd following the cable, untangle it off his red Doc Martens, and fight my way back up on stage.

The band's playing "Holiday in Cambodia." Biafra has tied himself to the mic stand with the cable, the remainder wrapped around his eyes like a blindfold. His body spasmodically jerks, mimicking being shot by a firing squad. Biafra's clothes are soaked with sweat. When he lifts his hands in the air, liquid sweat pours out of his green surgical gloves.

The stage is drenched, making it slippery as hell and difficult to maneuver as I try not to fall on my face. A beer can appears out of nowhere and flies past my head. With the low ceilings, the stage lighting is barely three feet above us. If something gets thrown from the crowd, I can't see it coming, and then it magically materializes when it breaks through the spotlight's glare. Giving me milliseconds to duck out of the way.

A beautiful girl with a huge mohawk stands pressed against the stage by the PA cabinets. Whenever I'm on that side our eyes meet, and she smiles. When I was in the pit, she was next to me, and as I lifted myself back up onto the stage, she put her hands on my ass and shoved me forward. I'm thinking this is love, or at least lust, and when it looks like she's had enough of getting crushed by the crowd I reach down and pull her on stage. Folding into my arms, I lead her behind the gear, by the drum kit. We crouch together, I hand her a beer, she says thanks, but it's so loud I can only see her mouth the word.

I'm staring into her eyes when a stagediver crashes into the drum kit, knocking over the ride, floor toms, and mics. I right the cymbal, Mohawk Girl uprights the toms. I grab the kid, shoving him across the stage until he's airborne. When I get back, she's already got the mics in place. I reposition the kick mic, while hand signaling with D.H. to make sure everything is good.

Checking the rest of the band, I notice Ray pointing at his amp. I make my way around the drum kit and walk into a shoe flying through the air. It hits me square in the face. I'm momentarily stunned. I can't see. I'm in pain but keep moving. Ray says his Echoplex isn't working. I check the back of his amp. The foot pedal jack is hanging half out. I push it back in. He gives me the thumbs up. I crawl behind the drum kit and sit down. My head aches.

Mohawk Girl puts her arms around me and wipes the dirt on my face with her sleeve. I feel like a kid whose mom is cleaning him up with tissues and spit.

Ray hits the last chord, Klaus throws his bass into the middle of the stage, and the band walks off. I'm starting to hate Klaus tossing his bass at the end of every show. It bends the tuning pegs and fucks the neck up. But I have to admit it's cool as hell to have it lying there, droning feedback reverberating over the PA, as the crowd screams for more.

Mohawk Girl and I are standing off to the side of the stage. I've my arm around her. She turns and kisses me, biting my lower lip. I kiss her back, hard, my tongue in her mouth. She presses herself into me, grinding against my semi-hard cock. I grab her ass with both hands and pull her against me. Leaning in to kiss her neck, I feel her hand rubbing my jeans, stroking my dick. We stay together in each other's arms, groping and kissing.

The crowd erupts when the band comes back for an encore. I turn around letting go of the girl, and work the stage through two more songs, my hard-on pressing against my jeans for the first few minutes. When it's finally over and Klaus tosses his bass again, I catch it before it hits the ground. The band walks off and I begin breaking down the gear. Mohawk Girl is gone.

Everything is packed and the road cases are lined up by the backdoor. I do one last walk through of the dressing room to make sure nothing has been left. Out in the parking lot, Microwave and I load the gear into the van. It's a puzzle that only fits one way, and when I put the bass cabinet in, I realize I fucked up and start taking it apart to do it over again. I'm pissed and tired and I want to get out of here. I've a motel room and want to get some sleep and take a shower. There's no show tomorrow, we've a day off.

Closing the rear doors, I walk around to the front of the van and Mohawk Girl is sitting in the passenger's seat.

"Hey," I say.

She smiles. I smile back and pull out a pack of cigarettes. I'm no longer in a hurry. But Microwave is. He gets in the driver's seat and starts the van.

"Getting in?" he says.

The motel is a few miles away, out by the highway. We pass a few other decent-looking motels and then turn into a disheveled one-story motor court, no frills, dingy and gray without a pool. We pull up in front of a row of numbered doors. D.H. and Biafra are walking towards us, suitcases in hand.

"They're all in a row," says Microwave.

"What do you mean?" says Biafra.

"We've six rooms, all in a row, starting with 10."

I'm thinking six rooms. Thank god, that means the promoter has gotten us all singles, and I'm not bunking with Microwave. I reach behind Mohawk Girl to get my bag.

"Come on," I tell her.

The motel room is way worse than most of the cheap motels promoters put us in. The queen-sized bed's comforter has cigarette burns, there are no chairs, the lamp on the nightstand's bulb is missing, there's a faded spot on the wall where the bad framed art used to be, and the TV is bolted to the top of a chest of drawers.

"Back in a sec."

I drop my bag, grab the plastic ice bucket, and go outside to the van. There're two cases of warm beers stashed with the gear. I take six and walk over to the ice machine on the other side of the parking lot by the office.

When I get back to the room, the TV is on and the overhead light is off. Mohawk Girl is naked in bed, partially covered by sheets, illuminated by the TV's bluish glow. She's sitting up, propped against the pillows, definitely striking a pose. Her back is arched, her breasts sticking almost straight out, inviting. I put down the beers and unbuckle my belt.

Naked, I slip under the sheets and crawl on top of her. Kissing her lips, I work my way down to her nipples. When I press my hard cock inside, she digs her nails into my ass, and roughly pulls me in. I grab her wrists and hold her down on the bed as I slam my cock in and then pull it out, over and over.

Her eyes are wide open and she's staring at me, I lean down to kiss her, and she shoves me away, pulls me out, and turns around. On her knees, she looks over her shoulder and reaches between her legs. In her hand is a small bottle of lubricant. She yanks my dick, hard.

"In my ass," she says, and puts her head down as I slowly press inside, a low moan escaping her lips. I grab her shoulders and pull her back, towards me, my cock to the hilt in her ass. Slowly, we begin moving together. Out and back in, I grip her hips, pulling, pushing. When I thrust in, she shoves back, our rhythm picks up, and we move faster—a slapping sound when my body hit hers. I feel it building inside of me. I don't want to cum yet. I want to stay in this very moment, fucking her.

I reach between her thighs and finger her clit. She's bucking, shoving backwards, our bodies slamming against one another. She is soaking wet, my fingers slide, she moans, and I shoot a load inside of her. We both collapse and fall asleep.

Someone's knocking on the door. I raise my head and turn to look. One of Mohawk Girl's spikes stabs my eye and I yell. It fucking hurts and my eye tears up. The TV is still on. The room dark. A sliver of sunshine is visible between the closed drapes. I get up and walk to the door.

"Yeah?"

"Maid service."

Thinking this wasn't a motel that actually had maid service, I'd forgotten to hang the "Do Not Disturb" sign.

"No thanks."

A single beer floats in the ice bucket. I open it, take a drink, and get back in bed. On the nightstand, there's a pack of cigarettes and I light one. The digital alarm clock reads 9:17AM. I prop a pillow and lean against the headboard.

Mohawk Girl is asleep. Her face burrowed in the pillow, a wet patch by her mouth. Her lips slightly parted as she breathes. She's young and beautiful and I feel like shit for fucking her. I've a girlfriend in San Francisco. A girlfriend I love. A girlfriend I feel guilty cheating on. But I do it anyway. I do it a lot. Every time, just like now, I feel like a piece of shit. Yet knowing I will always feel this guilt and shame never stops me.

I chug the beer. On the TV, a newscaster is yammering on about yesterday's elections in Nicaragua, "The first free elections in fifty-six years, and the Sandinistas are winning with over sixty percent..."

I get up and turn the TV off. Stub my cigarette in the ashtray and finish the beer. The room is dark and comfortable. It's the end of the tour and the idea of getting back in the van and driving the 1,800 miles to S.F. isn't very appealing.

WATCHA GONNA DO?
1984: SAN FRANCISCO

Coming home is always bittersweet. I love living in San Francisco. I just don't want to deal with the realities of life—paying bills, a relationship, and responsibilities. Being on the road is perfect. I drop into people's lives when I want, and just as easily leave without saying goodbye.

For Anna Lisa, it's not as easy. I'm not very supportive when I'm on tour. I don't help pay rent. I'm here and then I'm gone. She's strung-out and the difficulties of maintaining a heroin habit have gotten her in trouble. Drug dealers are calling all day and night wanting their money. Friends are pissed that she shorted them on drug deals or outright never gave them the drugs they paid for. She owes everyone dumb enough to lend her cash.

When I get back all of these people expect me to do something, make it right. Everyone knows I'm working so they think I have money. But I've spent most of it on drugs while on the road and what's left is barely enough to keep me well before I leave on another tour.

It's so bad Anna Lisa can't buy from most of the dealers we know, and she's been forced to score on the street, which is a whole other level of drug use and not a very good one. The local dope spot is only a few blocks away from Mission A. Now the dealers are hanging around and knocking on the front door asking Anna Lisa if they can use her room to shoot up and sell drugs.

A pair of women dealers are always around. She's doing them favors. Cutting their hair for a quarter gram. Letting them use her phone. It's a bust waiting to happen. I tell her to be careful. But, at the same time, I'm buying drugs from them because it's convenient. I'm a hypocrite. Why should Anna Lisa listen to me?

Now when I walk through the neighborhood all these dealers know my name. I used to be known as "that punk rock white boy." It's getting way too familiar. I'm not sure what to do about. But I'm too strung-out and loaded to care.

THE WAY OF THE WORLD
1984/1985: FLIPPER

After middle-manning a piece of heroin, I hit the Uptown on 17th and Capp, hoping to go unnoticed, and shoot up in the bathroom. Will Shatter is drinking at the bar. He says hello like we're old friends. I'm wondering what he's doing in the Mission when he lives with Brenda in my old apartment in North Beach. I'm hoping he's looking to score. Turns out he's not and we just start talking. Feels like a million years since I was with Brenda and I'm way past having resentments. Or maybe I'm just high and whatever feelings I might still have are dulled.

Will says he's starting a new band called A3I (Any Three Initials) with Emilio from Bad Posture and two other guys I don't know. He invites me down to the first show at the On Broadway. We shake hands. I say goodbye.

A few months later Will calls and asks me to road manage Flipper's next tour. I meet the band at Capp Street Studios. It's a monster tour, even for Flipper, stretching well over two months with Christmas and New Year's Eve in New York City. Their second album *Gone Fishin'* has just been released on the Subterranean label and the band is touring behind it. It'll be the classic original Flipper lineup: Will Shatter (bass/vocals), Bruce Loose (bass/vocals), Ted Falconi (guitar), and Steve DePace (drums).

We're standing around the '56 International Harvester delivery truck that Flipper uses to tour. The truck is covered in graffiti. One whole side has "Flipper Suffered for Their Sins, Now It's Your Turn" and "Coming to a Repair Shop Near You." I'm thinking about the redneck truck stops in Wyoming or driving in the Deep South. I'm calculating the fines and traffic stops and the fact we're all carrying and doing drugs and possibly getting busted.

"We gotta paint the truck," I say.

Bruce's girlfriend, Paula, is glaring at me. "You're not a real road manger." She smiles and tugs on Bruce's arm. "I could be the road manager. You should take me instead."

I'm not sure why she needs to say that. I'm self-conscious and immediately don't like her. Besides, everyone knows girlfriends and tours don't mix. But DePace agrees and goes out and buys a couple gallons of flat black paint and a portable sprayer. We spend the next two hours painting the truck.

"Sacrilege." Will shakes his head and opens another beer.

"You better be worth it." Ted is pissed and won't help paint.

Wanting to cover the graffiti is just being practical, which is something that isn't very Flipper. Although to save money, they aren't hiring a roadie. Everyone will be doing double-duty loading the gear, which is financially practical, so there is that. Problem is it's just going to be them and me in the truck. We haven't even left yet and I'm already starting to regret taking this tour.

***

Doesn't matter how much you take with you. You always run out. But this is ridiculous. We just played our first show, and Will and I are already out of dope. It's fucking Denver. All I've ever scored in this town were a dozen Klonopins at an Arby's on Broadway. And I only bought them because I couldn't find heroin.

Tomorrow's a day off and we're stuck in the motel staring at the TV. It's December and cold as hell. Neither of us wants to wander around in search of drugs. Only, we're both starting to get dope sick. Three weeks ago, I'd tried to wean myself off. Tapering down. Using less. Hoping I could somehow avoid withdrawals and be clean for tour. But all I really was doing was chipping and I still have a habit. Apparently, Will wasn't even doing that. He's drinking a beer, a Chesterfield hanging from his lips, looking like a handsome corpse. Will does dope sick like nobody else I know. He doesn't let it get to him, whereas I want to just die. Will's up and working on finding drugs.

Last night at the show, we'd met this cool chick. Both of us were talking to her. She had hung around backstage. I kind of dug her. She had a cool artist vibe. Like she should be in New York or San Francisco, not stuck up here in the Rockies. I'm not sure if I was imagining it or not but it felt as if she was digging on me. Only, she's not someone I thought could score drugs. But Will's on the phone with her. And I'm thinking, *How the fuck did he get her number?* With his hand over the receiver, Will whispers that she knows a dude that can get Dilaudids.

DePace wasn't too cool with us just going off on our own. "Make sure you're back here by 8:30. Otherwise we're leaving ya," which is total bullshit. Sure, they could leave me and do all right. But Will's the talent. Nobody is going anywhere without him.

We're in a taxi heading over to her house. I have no idea where we are. I don't really know Denver and this part of town seems to be out in the boonies. The streets are numbered and there are goddamn trees everywhere. Her house is tucked away off the street and overgrown with bushes. We're in the country. I fucking hate the country.

She greets us at the door, dressed in fifties chic, a drink in one hand, a cigarette in the other. She gives me a hug and lingers when brushing her lips along my cheek. If I wasn't in complete withdrawal and about to run off to the bathroom to simultaneously hurl and shit my pants, I'd be more responsive to her advances.

Will and I are sitting in her living room. She's in the kitchen making drinks. She offered scotch and soda. We both took her up on it.

"Man, she's hitting on you."

"I can't remember her name."

Will tells me her name. I immediately forget it.

"She's got a kid," I say.

"So?" says Will. "Kid's not here right now, is he?"

Two hours later we're still waiting for her friend to show up with the pills.

"Is he coming?" I ask for the third time. The scotch having left a nasty taste in my mouth has my insides churning. I'm profusely sweating and at the same time freezing.

"Not feeling well?" she says. Obviously, she doesn't understand what being dope sick entails. But she's super nice and doing us this giant favor. I try and relax. Wait it out.

It's almost midnight when her friend shows. He takes one look at us and knows what we're about. When he pulls out a small prescription bottle and dumps four pills onto the coffee table, I'm disappointed to see they're orange two milligram pills, not the four milligram yellow ones.

"Twenty-five a piece," he says.

This is highway robbery. Anywhere else they'd be going for, at the most, five to ten dollars. I want to throttle this scumbag. Will just shrugs and pulls out his money.

I'm in the bathroom. I had to borrow a spoon from her kitchen to cook the dope. Crushing both the pills into a powder, I pour them in and add water, running my lighter back and forth under the spoon as the cloudy liquid clears. Ripping off a piece of cigarette filter, I drop it in, press in the tip of the needle, and draw up the orange liquid. Tying off, I find a vein, and stick the needle into my arm. When I pull it out, a trickle of blood runs down and drips onto the black and white tile floor.

There is nothing like the rush of drugs hitting your system when you've been sick. Warmth runs through your entire body. The withdrawal symptoms are immediately gone. The panic in your brain finally subsides. I don't want to move. Just want to sit here, on the toilet, in this moment forever.

Rinsing the rig, I spray the red-tinted water into the sink. All over the floor are her kid's toys. A plastic battleship and a rubber ducky are mixed in with shampoos and creme rinse. Pair of nylons and underwear are hanging off the shower curtain pole. The normalcy of this scene quickly reminds me of where I am. I quickly clean up, wiping the blood off the sink and floor with toilet paper. Flushing the toilet, I avoid looking in the mirror. I don't want to see myself invading the sanctity of this woman's bathroom.

Will's on the couch nodded out. It's two in the morning. We should be getting back to the motel. It's 6AM when we finally leave. The cab is waiting for us. Neither of us says a word, other than to tell the driver where we're going.

The sun's just about to rise when we arrive at the motel. DePace and Ted are up and packing. Bruce is still asleep. DePace is pissed. "Where the fuck you guys been?" We ignore him and pack our gear. The motel room is warm. I light a cigarette and stare out the window at the gray dawn.

"Denver's not so bad," I say.

"You're just fucking loaded," says Will.

Ted's been driving for hours while the rest of us sleep. He eventually pulls over in a dimly lit rest stop and roughly wakes me. "You're the road manager. Your turn to drive."

I shake off the Dilaudid numb and get out of bed. It's cold as hell. I've never driven this truck. I sit in the driver's seat and check the rearview mirrors and rev the motor. It's a stick shift with four on the floor and a low gear ratio that's awesome for hills, but stressfully slow for highway travel. In the back, there's a large platform bed that sleeps three and underneath, accessible from the rear doors, is a storage area where we keep the gear. Along the wall behind me is another bench seat that doubles as a bed. And then there's a fold-out "helper's chair" across from me that Ted is now sitting in.

As I pull out of the rest stop, Ted starts rummaging around and setting up some contraption on the floor between us.

"What the fucks that?"

"Want an espresso?"

Ted's got a small butane camping stove and an ancient, battered Italian Bialetti stovetop espresso maker. He fills the Bialetti with finely ground coffee and water from a plastic gallon jug. When he lights the stove, there's a loud hiss.

"That shit gonna blow up?"

"Not if you drive right."

It's the dead of winter and the sky is a dark black-blue in contrast to the bluish snow-covered hills and fields. There's a sliver of a moon and a ton of stars reaching across the horizon. It's eerily beautiful in its bleak grandiose-ness. When the smell of coffee hits the air, I'm ready for a cup. But of course there's no milk and the espresso is insanely bitter.

I reach for my bag and get out a pack of smokes, my Walkman, and headphones. With the cigarette lit, I cue the Walkman and start to put on the headphones.

"You can't wear those," says Ted as he sips his coffee and stares out at the passing snow-covered fields.

"Why not?"

"You won't be able to hear the engine. Might over-rev, blow it up."

"Excuse me?"

"You have to be able to hear the motor when you drive. Be in sync with the engine."

"Man, come on Ted. That's fucking crazy."

"Hey, my truck, my tour, my rules."

***

Flipper just played the Jockey Club in Newport, Kentucky—
an old speakeasy left over from the prohibition era. On the walls
were photos of all the bands that have played there: Frank Sinatra,
The Isley Brothers with Jim Hendrix on guitar, Muddy Waters, and
even Johnny Cash. It's a club full of good old boys and the whiskey
was flowing. They offered us a motel but we've a show in
Washington, DC and have to drive all night to get there.

Bruce and Will want to go to a party across the Ohio River in
Cincinnati. I'm shit-faced drunk and couldn't give a shit. Ted and
DePace are also drunk, but still want to get on the road. Bruce and
Will ignore all of us and drive the truck to a warehouse, get out, and
leave. Ted is pissed off and lies down in the back. Steve's passed out.
At one point in the show, I'd brought him shots and poured them
down his throat while he played.

I'm sitting in the driver's seat, melancholic and depressed.
I'm twenty-nine years old. I don't have shit. I'm strung-out and on
tour with Flipper. I can barely buy a pack of smokes. I hate my life.
Yet the focus of all my misery becomes the wrong Will did when he
stole Brenda. The fact that I wasn't happy when I was with her
doesn't matter. On the drive from the club, I told Will he fucked up
my life. I was slurring my words, cussing him out. It's all that damn
free whiskey the promoter gave us, and really this is old news.

Will looked confused, gave Bruce a "what the fuck"
expression, and told me to get over it.

"Go to sleep, Patrick," said Bruce.

"Fuck you."

Now they're off at a party and I'm stewing in my self-pity.
It's well past 3AM. We don't have time for this shit. We need to be
on the road.

The wind blows through the pine trees as I drag myself out of
the truck, zip up my leather, and search for the entrance to the

warehouse. It's a huge brick building on a hill with a lot of trees and it appears deserted. I hear music and wander into a large empty room with scaffolding along one wall and sheets of dirty plastic draped from the high ceilings. A single lightbulb hangs by a wire in the middle of the room, its harsh light creating shadows, a perfect location for a slasher film. In a loft off the main room, I find Bruce and Will with two girls drinking beers.

"Come on, man. We gotta go."

"Don't stress it, road manager."

"Seriously man, we got a long drive."

"Still crying about Brenda?"

"No, I'm done."

"Finally."

"Fuck you."

"I'm starving. Let's hit Waffle House."

There is something magically depraved about Waffle House. From the yellow squares with black-lettered signs, to the inebriated all-night patrons and unapologetically unhealthy menu. You know you're in the South when you start seeing Waffle House signs towering above the gas stations along the highway—not a place where you'd order a salad. It's strictly carbs, grease, meat, sugar, and a bottomless cup of coffee, not to be mistaken as in the same league as IHOP or Denny's. Waffle House is on its own level and no doubt responsible for the South's penchant for obesity and diabetes.

The signs on I-95 point us toward the Holland Tunnel and New York City. For the next three weeks, it'll be our home base. We're playing an all-ages show at CBGB's and New Year's Eve at the Pyramid. The out-of-town shows—Boston, Toronto, and New Jersey—are relatively easy drives.

We're staying with Denise Ondayko (guitar/vocals: Hexis Plex) at her apartment on 3rd Street across from the Hells Angels building. It's the former residence of Susan Miller (guitar: Frightwig, Tanks, Bad Posture), and I'm gathering that Flipper's open invite to stay here was sort of grandfathered in from when Susan held the lease.

The apartment is in a dank, windowless basement that was probably the utility area where the building super hung out back in the day. It's a warren of small brick alcoves. The bathroom and kitchen are tiny and definitely not up to code. Only in N.Y.C. would this be called an apartment.

We park the truck. Our California plates elicit stares from the Angels posted up in front of their building guarding the bikes and keeping an eye on the neighborhood. They watch us unloading luggage and seem confused. "Hey, where in California you from?"

"San Francisco."

"Cool. Careful with your truck. Lot of criminals around here."

I'm not sure what to make of that last statement. The Hells Angels block is one of the safest on the Lower East Side. Unless of course they don't like you and then you're fucked. I'm hoping it's just a friendly warning that vehicles aren't safe anywhere in Manhattan.

"Gonna have to take turns sleeping in the truck," says Ted.

"What?"

"You heard me."

"I'm not sleeping in the fuckin' truck."

"Somebody's gotta watch the gear."

"Your truck. Your gear. Your rules."

***

CBGB's is packed. It's not a big club and can get claustrophobic when sold out. But hey, it's CBGB's. There's so much history, who cares if you can't move or breath? I push through the crowd toward the stage and run into 4-Way (Singer: Bad Posture) and his wife Gloria and introduce myself again. We've met before, but that was years ago. We all hang out together while Flipper plays their set. Unlike the Kennedys, I don't work stage for Flipper. Flipper can take care of themselves.

I once watched Ted completely annihilate a kid while Flipper was playing at the Eastern Front in the East Bay. They were performing outside on a stage with no back railing or light tresses. The band was out in the open, there were a ton of stage divers, and this kid got too close behind Ted and he freaked. Swinging his guitar, he bashed the kid in the head. The crowd went ape shit. Punks were throwing cans and bottles and screaming. When the commotion calmed down, Ted walked to the mic, "You get on my stage while I'm playing, and I treat you like an adult."

I'm out front after the show with 4-Way and Gloria. A crowd has formed and we're practically yelling at each other just to have a conversation. Gloria shouts that Sheri, Ted's girlfriend, is coming to N.Y.C. for the Christmas holidays and New Year's. I have to ask her to repeat what she said. This is the first I've heard of Sheri's plans. But then Ted isn't exactly communicative. Sheri and Ted's relationship can get volatile. So, this isn't exactly good news.

***

The holidays suck. It's not like I actually celebrate Christmas. I've never owned a Christmas tree. I don't bake a ham or decorate cookies. On New Year's Eve, I'm always working at some fucking club. If I even remember it's Thanksgiving, I order an open-face turkey sandwich with gravy and mashed potatoes at 2AM in some shithole truck stop where the waitress is sneaking shots of JD and the short order cook smokes a Marlboro while preparing my food.

I'm never with family on the holidays. The band might take a few days off to go home. But I'm stuck on the road with the gear, T-shirts, and my depression—and I really wouldn't have it any other way. So I'm sort of at odds when my sister, Scott, invites me out to her place on City Island for Christmas Eve. Don't get me wrong. I love my sister. But what she doesn't know, and I'd like to keep it that way, is I'm a strung-out junkie.

New York City is heroin mecca. When I'm there, I'm in full-blown junkie mode. The dealers sell ten-dollar glassine bags and there's a street full of folks peddling blue cap hypodermic needles twenty-four hours a day. I fucking love the Lower East Side. It's dope-fiend Disneyland.

"Come out for dinner. Stay the night," she says. "It'll be fun."

"But I got the band with me."

"Bring them along. No one should be alone during the holidays."

I tell Flipper I'm going out to my sister's and invite them to come along. DePace says no. I'm catching attitude from him for doing drugs. While our relationship has never been what you'd call close, we're starting to not even be friends. Besides, Flipper doesn't have any shows for this entire week. We've just been sitting around. Fuck him if I'm getting high. Ted, who always tends to side with DePace, acts like he doesn't hear me. I know Sheri is here, so I don't press it. Bruce and Will are just as bored as I am and say yeah.

My sister's boyfriend, Neil Kraft, picks us up in his car. We're totally loaded, and the conversation is disjointed to say the least. There're long moments of silence that Will does his best to avoid by asking Neil what he does for a living and talking about the shitty traffic. We're on the Cross Bronx Expressway, I'm nodding and scratching my nose, and Neil says, "You're scratching like a junkie, Patrick." Bruce and Will start laughing. I'm self-conscious and beginning to think this definitely wasn't a good idea.

My sister gives us all hugs—always the perfect host. Will is his charming self. Bruce is on his best behavior. We make a huge dinner of chili rellenos and tacos. Scott shopped at the only Mexicatessen in the city that makes fresh tortillas. After over a month on the road, it's amazing to have home-cooked food.

Before we eat, we make a toast with beers and wine and laugh. My sister tells me she loves me and misses me. Afterwards we all help with the dishes, and then say our goodnight. Will and Bruce take the couches in the living room. I get the guest room.

I'm cooking a shot in the bathroom and catch a glimpse of myself in the mirror. I'm gaunt, hollow face, my hair is a disheveled mess, and my skin is gray. I'm a fucking liar. I'm a junkie. I'm the worse piece of shit brother. I want to run out of my sister's house. Instead, I do the shot and crawl into bed.

Three years later after Anna Lisa attempts suicide and my entire family discovers we're junkies, Anna Lisa will go off to rehab and I'll head out to New York to try and clean up. This may sound like insanity as N.Y.C. is heroin central, but Scott offers to let me stay at her new house in the Bronx and help them renovate. But only if I stay clean. This of course is what 12 steppers call "doing a geographic," which basically means moving your addiction to another locale. Only there's another saying, "Everywhere you go, there you are." I might have been away from the familiar territory of my dealers in S.F., but I'm still that junkie looking to get loaded. But, for the most part, I actually do stop shooting dope. Only problem is I drink myself to death every night and I'm depressed as hell.

I didn't know what "getting clean" really meant. I'd been to a few AA meetings, and I thought them lame. But then I thought anyone who didn't do drugs was lame. My perception was if you had to quit you were weak, and besides, who were you really hurting? Nobody but yourself, right? Why should anyone care?

At the end of the year, I move back to California. Within months I'm strung-out again.

City Gardens in Trenton, New Jersey is a "legendary" shithole that everybody has played. A rickety building that looks more like a condemned warehouse than a nightclub. The promoter is a guy named Randy Ellis who calls himself Randy Now. I've been here with T.S.O.L. and never quite got the charm.

"You'se guys want me to order some pies?" shouts Randy.

The greasy pizza is phenomenal. But the mood backstage is down. We've played twelve shows in twenty days and driven three thousand miles. Everyone is tired, on each other's nerves, and this tour isn't even half over yet.

I stuff another slice of pizza in my mouth as Anna Lisa walks into the dressing room. I knew she was coming after Christmas but didn't expect her to show up here in New Jersey. But her flight was changed and arrived early. Instead of waiting for us, she jumped on Amtrak and taxied from the train station. Now, Will and I are not so down but DePace goes ape shit. "I know you got drugs," he yells at Anna Lisa. "Don't get them loaded, they've both been doing so well."

I'm not really sure what DePace is referring to. I don't know how "well" either of us has been doing. We've been shooting dope every day, drunk at every show, and scamming any drugs we could get our hands on. DePace, the de facto band manager, is always somewhat delusional and makes up stories in his head that he can live with. How else could you survive in a band like Flipper?

Twelve years from now, I hook up with DePace's niece at the end of my using career. Strung-out and desperate, I'll turn to armed robbery to pay for our habits. DePace will blame me for dragging her down. She's half my age and I blame myself too. When the cops kicked in my door to arrest me, they will bust her as well. I'll tell the cops that the drugs are mine and they let her go. She'll visit me in county jail, and I'll tell her she's got to move on. I'm looking at twenty-five to life, and I'm not getting out anytime soon.

DePace will never talk to me again. Behind my back, he tells everyone that he's going to kick my ass. After I get out on parole, I never go back to work in the music scene. But as an author, I do readings at punk shows and there are gigs he cancels because I'm on the bill. At a party, at the performance artist Johanna West's house in Los Angeles for Frightwig's reunion show, he'll run out the back door just to avoid me.

As soon as DePace is gone, we all head to the bathroom. The rush from the dope is intensely strong. I get a great nod and miss most of the show. After the audience has left, Will is still up on stage. He's leaning against the mic stand with a finger in one ear, clearly nodding away. A few people who work at the club and some musicians from other bands are laughing. I help him off stage and we run into Ted.

"Those fuckers slashed our tire!"

"What? Who you talkin' about?"

"Fucking Scorn Flakes."

"Who?"

This is one of the biggest problems, in an array of many problems, working for a band like Flipper. You have no idea what damage they may have caused on previous tours. The local New Jersey band Scorn Flakes is on a vendetta and out for revenge. Last time they were on the bill with Flipper, some of their gear went missing. They blame Flipper, most specifically Bruce. Flipper denies anything was ever taken. Now the Scorn Flakes have slashed our truck's tire.

I confront a couple of the guys from Scorn Flakes. But I really don't know them or what transpired last time. They're pissed off, sarcastic, and talk a lot of shit. I don't like them, but then I don't like a lot of people. Rather than continue to argue, I call a tow truck. Our International Harvester is nearly thirty years old and a commercial vehicle. The tires have split rims that require hydraulic tools to remove the locking ring that holds them in place. It's not something we can do ourselves. This adds to the cost of the repair and takes a bite out of our dwindling funds.

As we wait in the nearly deserted, weed-choked parking lot, the Scorn Flakes lean against their car loudly talking shit. I'm hoping we can get out of here without getting into a physical altercation. A cop car circles the block, gives us the once over, decides we're not worthy of harassing, and drives off. The Scorn Flakes eventually get bored and leave. We smoke a lot of cigarettes and wait. Two hours later the tire is fixed, and we head back to the city.

***

It's New Year's Eve and we're playing the Pyramid Club. It's cold and I can feel it even though I've an overcoat and the leather jacket underneath. We've loaded in the gear as snow flurries filled the sky. Two hours later we finished sound check, and everyone is hanging at the bar where it's warm. There are two opening bands and New Year's Eve before we play. The bartenders are incredibly generous giving out drinks to the band. I'm in the corner of the bar with Bruce, Will, and Anna Lisa.

I've a nod going and I'm nursing my drink. Yesterday we scored a couple bundles of dope with the brand name 357 Magnum. A bundle is ten bags sold at a retail price break. In N.Y.C., heroin comes in ten dollar glassine bags, folded up small with a brand name printed on the side. There is so much out there on the streets it's a little scary.

Sheri shows up looking like a punk rock bag lady. She says, "Hi," and hugs everyone. Sheri is a whirlwind of energy. She's talking a mile a minute and Ted immediately disappears. I'm so deep in my nod I can't deal with her being so tweaked out.

I go back to drinking at the bar. Sheri and Anna Lisa get into a fight. They're screaming at each other and Anna Lisa storms out of the club. It's some bullshit about Anna Lisa's ex who's a friend of Sheri's. But really Sheri is just trying to cause drama. Speed freaks tend to do that.

I'm about to go after Anna Lisa, and I really don't want to, and then it's midnight. Everyone in the club is screaming and the band has to go on stage and play.

DePace says, "Happy New Year!"

I'm totally pissed off and tell him to go fuck himself.

"Fuck you too!" he says.

After the show we pack the gear and start to load out. The stage manager opens the front door and outside the entire street and sidewalk is blanketed with ten inches of pristine white snow. We all walk out into the middle of Avenue A. There are no cars or buses and it's eerily quiet and beautiful. The snow continues to fall and the city looks like a winter wonderland. It's so peaceful that it's hard to believe we're in the Lower East Side.

Ted and Sheri wander off, leaving two sets of footprints in the white snow down the middle of the street. DePace isn't speaking to me and tells Will he'll drive the truck back to the apartment. Bruce is nowhere around. Will and I walk home.

Hopefully, Anna Lisa will be there. But really this is typical of our relationship. There are periodic blowouts and then we make up only to never talk about it.

The next day, Anna Lisa flies home. Sheri sticks around a little longer. I don't really interact with her as she has a ton of speed and I'd rather just numb out on heroin and not be interrupted by tweakers. Ted and Sheri are always over at Gloria and 4-Way's on 2nd Ave. Bruce, Will, DePace, and I hold up at Denise's place, huddled around an ancient space heater. The beautiful white snow has turned gray. The sidewalks are iced over and dangerous to walk on. The temperature has dropped to freezing. Grumpy New Yorkers trudge off to work, the peaceful beauty of last night's snowfall all but a memory.

***

I'm back at The Channel in Boston and Flipper just played an early all-ages show. The club manager is the same Goodfella wannabe from when I was here with Subhumans. Unlike last time, however, we get paid in full.

My father, Wayne, who lives in Boston, and his girlfriend, Maya, show up and offer to take us all out to dinner at a Thai restaurant they really like. In fact, it's their favorite restaurant and the owner knows them. When the waiter sees them and that we're a large party, he sets up five small tables in a row down the middle of the room.

This is a nice restaurant with large potted plants, bent cane furniture, white linen tablecloths, and candles on the tables. Behind us, there's a middle-aged couple holding hands and kissing every few minutes, practically making out. In my mind, I write the story they're rediscovering their love for one another. For all I know, it could just be a first date.

From the minute we sit down, there's a sense that this isn't going to go right. Idle chitchat isn't Flipper's forte. The conversation is rough and midway into dinner it all starts going even more south. Bruce and Ted exchange harsh words regarding the selling of a Fender bass amp that the group had communally bought for touring. The implication is that it was sold so Bruce and/or Will could buy drugs. Ted is pissed. Halfway out of his chair, he cusses everyone out, and the sheer violence of his response is unsettling. When he sits down, he apologizes and then begins telling Wayne and Maya of his military service in Vietnam. They get very quiet. The argument, having never quite finished, starts up again. The volume goes up a notch. Dishes are thrown. There's food spilled all over the table, a broken wine glass, forks and spoons on the floor. DePace yells, "Shut the fuck up!" Everyone responds, "Fuck you." The other customers are either staring or talking about us. The middle-aged couple hastily pays their bill and runs out the door.

I'm so desensitized from having lived with Flipper for the last few months that this behavior hardly bothers me. I finish my plate of pad thai, look around for my beer, and realize it's on the floor. The owner brings our check, indicating he wants us to leave.

After dinner, we say our goodbyes, pile in the truck, and drive south to N.Y.C.

Wayne and Maya never go back to that restaurant.

***

Our New York "residency" is finally over and the tour heads west towards home. We've driven down the East Coast and played a few shows at some smaller venues, the crowds aren't materializing, and the money isn't what we hoped. At one dismal show in Charlotte, North Carolina, the promoter absolutely rips us off, paying us practically nothing. He and I get into a shouting match. I'm about to kick his ass when Ted pulls me away. There are cops at the door watching us. More specifically, they're watching me.

The truth is the lack of shows over the holidays and hanging around N.Y.C. for three weeks has depleted our cash reserve. We really needed to make some money just to pay for gas. I tell the band we're in financial trouble. Ted says they could just stop paying me. Tempers flare, the lack of money causing friction.

"What's your deal?" asks Bruce.

"My deal?"

"Yeah. I'm on tour because I'm a musician, this is what I do, and touring sucks. What's you're excuse?"

At this exact moment, I really don't have an answer for Bruce.

***

We're at the 688 Club in Atlanta for two shows; an early "all-ages" show for the underage punks, and then there's a twenty-one and over show. A lot of punk clubs and promoters do this, as it's "politically correct," but it's not like we're getting paid for playing two complete shows. We do a little better than just one show, but if you think about it, two performances in one night are excessively grueling for the band—especially for a band that's touring—and this is just another stop on a road full of many stops.

A lot of bands would go through the motions for the early show and then kill the later show, or maybe vice versa. But the one thing about Flipper is they're not just any band. As their graffiti says, "Flipper Rules, Don't Be Stupid." The first show is nothing short of incredible. When Flipper is on, it's electrifying, and this is one of those shows. I have never heard them play better. When you attend a Flipper show, it's a crapshoot as to what you'll get. Some nights they are just a bunch of noise, more interested in fucking with the audience than playing music. In L.A., after getting booed and harassed by an audience of hardcore punks waiting for the headliner, they played "Sex Bomb," a song that's sole lyrics consist of repeating, "She's a sex bomb, My baby—yeah," for an hour straight as the spit and trash rained down. Laughing the whole time.

Tonight, DePace's drums and Bruce's and Will's bass are in prefect sync. Ted's guitar work builds waves of feedback and tonal intonations. Bruce's vocals for "Sacrifice" give me goose bumps. Will tosses out an emotion-filled version of "Shine" like it was effortless. The kids go crazy and two hours later Flipper does it again with the late show. I get the feeling I'm witnessing history.

At load-out, the band is understandably exhausted. We've just put all the gear in the truck and then Bruce comes out of the club.

"I just called Tupper. He bought me a plane ticket home. I gotta go."

"Don't do that," says Will.

"Fuck!" DePace is pissed.

After our time in New York, none of us are getting along. The drug use has gotten out of control (as if it could ever be under control). No one wants to hang out together and we've become two factions: Ted and DePace, against Will and me. Bruce plays along with whoever has the most sway at any given moment. But now Bruce is having problems with his girlfriend, Paula, and he's more concerned with getting back to S.F. and saving his relationship.

"I can play bass," I say.

Before we even drop Bruce off at the airport, DePace is huddled in a phone booth making his own collect call to Steve Tupper, the founder of Flipper's label, Subterranean Records, trying to salvage the tour. After a short negotiation with a lot of yelling on DePace's part, Tupper agrees to fly out Bruno "De Smartass" DeMartis (guitar: Slug Lords, Bad Posture). Bruno played bass for Flipper on a previous tour that Will didn't make. The replacement should be seamless and we're back on the road.

I'm resentful when none of them even consider my offer to fill in for Bruce. It's not like I couldn't play Flipper's entire catalog in my sleep, having heard it nonstop for the last two months. But then I'd be doing double duty as a band member/road manager, and it'd be a pain in the ass taking care of the business end which is actually the main reason bands have managers. The good news is we got paid well tonight and we're finally not hurting for money.

***

It's an unusually warm, muggy afternoon for January, even for Texas. The club, a small storefront on the industrial side of Houston, called Cabaret Voltaire, isn't our usual venue, even for Flipper.

A couple of self-professed "commies" dressed in army fatigues run the place. One resembles General Noriega; the other, a characterless sort with glasses, supposedly a college professor. The club looks like a co-op, or a drop-in center on the skids. In a corner, there are shelves filled with Mao's *Little Red Book* and old issues of *The Daily Worker*. Mismatched chairs and tables are strewn haphazardly around the edge of the room. A dilapidated stage and a small, inefficient sound system, the kind you'd find in a rehearsal space, take up the majority of the exposed brick back wall.

I ask the commies if this is really the PA we're to use. General Noriega says not to worry, just wait for the sound guy, "He'll be here any minute." Then he smiles like a complacent Buddha and tells us to take whatever we want, and gestures toward the books and newspapers. I shove a *Little Red Book* in my pocket, but I'm not really sure why. It's written in Chinese, and I can't read Chinese.

We load in, set up the gear, and wait. An hour later, the sound guy shows up and shoves a mic or two in the general direction of the amps. Soundcheck takes all of ten minutes, a nightmare of feedback and a white noise hiss. Something's not grounded. The vocals are tinny, the drums flat. The bass is all you can really hear.

"This sucks," I say, and everyone agrees.

The reality is this show is just a gas stop. We're going to make shit-all nothing. Except, we can eat, pay expenses, and have enough to get us to the next gig. Sometimes that's all you can ask for. I'm just hoping people will show up and these guys don't renege on our guarantee. But it's not looking good. They've already misrepresented the sound system. The club is in a desolate location on the wrong side of town. I have no sense whether or not they advertised. Who the fuck knows what tonight will be like?

But for now it's down time and we're all outside on the street standing around, bored which isn't good. A bored Flipper is a volatile animal.

Ted wanders off, only to stop a few doors down outside an auto repair shop and starts digging through some rusted body parts that are leaning against the wall. Steve and Bruno say "fuck it" and go back inside the club. Will and I are by the truck smoking cigarettes, arguing. I want to shoot the dope we have left from New Orleans. Will wants to wait until later. It's our last hit, at least until we find more.

Inside the truck, under the plywood bench behind the driver's seat, there's a storage compartment filled with bags of clothes, assorted tools, extra pairs of boots, winter coats, and Ted's single burner camp stove. There's also a 6.5mm Carcano rifle (the same type of gun Oswald was supposed to have used to kill Kennedy), an extra clip with ammo, and a fully loaded lever-action .30-30 Winchester.

On our days off, driving between shows, we'd stop at swap meets and flea markets. In the middle of the Arizona desert, we'd hit a huge swap meet. It felt lawless. There were bikers, desert nomads, and leather-skinned old women in short shorts and halter tops. Amid the turquoise jewelry and taxidermied Jackalopes were army surplus ammunitions and rifles, lots of rifles. Will bought the Carcano and I'd picked up the Winchester. I'm not even sure why I'd bought the gun. I'd been looking for a handgun, really, a nice .45 or something more menacing. But for fifty dollars it was a good deal and I bought it.

Stowed with the gear in the storage space under the back loft bed, accessible only from the rear doors, are several bags of fireworks we'd purchased in Tennessee. Not your everyday firecrackers. These are the real deal: six-inch rockets, Roman candles, cylindrical shell mortars—firing double and triple breaks—Halley's Comets, and M-80s.

It also goes without saying that there are drugs in the truck. I know there's heroin, although not much, and a few assorted pills. There may also be some speed, definitely a couple of rigs, and who knows what other paraphernalia.

It's safe to say we're a rolling bust, a cop's wet dream, the stereotypical fear of every small-town sheriff—drug-crazed punks with guns on an interstate crime spree.

Will opens the back door and reaches around until he finds what he's looking for. A "Whistling Artillery" rocket, which is an eight-inch cylinder full of gunpowder and various pyrotechnic chemicals that's attached to a four-foot stick you're supposed to stand upright and shoot into the sky while it whistles until it blows up.

Will holds it by the stick, lights the fuse with his Chesterfield, and fires it off in Ted's direction. The rocket screeches three feet off the ground, leaving a trail of sparks and the stench of burning gunpowder in its wake. When it slams into the wall beside Ted's head and explodes, the sound is startlingly loud and out of place.

Will and I both laugh. I grab a couple of Roman candles, light one, and point it at Ted. He's running towards us with his head down as red phosphorus balls of fire ricochet off of everything around him. The sidewalk, the buildings, the parked cars, all have scorch marks. Ted keeps on coming and Will and I, laughing like maniacs, take off running, clutching a few more rockets and Roman candles.

Part of the myth that surrounds Ted Falconi is he was in the army and served in Vietnam. Ted says he saw action. Everyone else says he was in the rear with the gear—a supply sergeant, or he worked for army intelligence or some other rank and file job. Because Ted's first name is Lawrence, we call him Sergeant Larry. No one really knows what the true story is. Although one time I did say something about wanting to rip a guy's jaw off and Ted asked me if I wanted to know how.

Bruno and Steve rush out of the club and start laughing when they see us running away from Ted. But everyone dives for cover when Will lets lose another rocket and it blows up in the club's doorway. Then we all get into it. Rockets, Roman candles, and M-80s going off in every direction. It's the Fourth of July in January—a small Armageddon of our making.

I'm behind a parked car, using it as cover, trying to get back around to the truck for more ammo, when a police car turns the corner at the end of the block. Ted is busy digging out a monster rocket and doesn't see the cop. I yell at him, but he doesn't hear me. He lights the rocket and runs around the side of the truck, looking for Will. When he sees the patrol car, he ducks back behind the truck and stuffs the smoking rocket under the mattress of the loft bed and closes the door.

I'm thinking there are guns in there. There're fireworks. The fucking dope is inside that truck. It's my last hit. I run over, open the door, and pull the rocket out from under the mattress just as the cop pulls up alongside of me. The rocket ignites and soars into the air, covering me in embers, and explodes above our heads. I look at my hand. It's scorched black. The cuff of my Levi's jacket is charred.

The cop, your typical-looking redneck in a cowboy hat, doesn't even roll down his window. He just glares at me, shakes his head, and drives off. I'm holding my hand, trying to see if it's really burnt as badly as it appears to be.

"Man, that don't look so good," says Will.

I'm hoping the commies have a first aid kit, but somehow, I doubt it. That would be too conventional. When I show them my hand and ask, they shake their heads and tell me there's a hospital a few miles away. "But it's a repressive corporate institution that only wants your money," says General Noriega. "They could give a fuck about the health of this nation!"

I'm by the truck nursing a warm beer. Earlier, I washed my hand and got most of the soot off. Miraculously, I'm not burned. But just to be sure I wasn't in shock and couldn't feel the pain, I shot the last hit of my dope. I'm loaded and feeling pretty good.

There's a bunch of kids hanging around in front of the club. Mohawks, leather jackets, spiked hair, and skateboards. Inside, the opening band sounds fucking terrible. Across the street, a group of skinheads are doing what skinheads do: push other people around and act stupid. One of the girls, she's skinny and very pregnant, comes walking in my direction. There's something familiar about her I can't place.

"Hey," she says.

"Hey," I say back.

"Long time, no see." She smiles up at me as she sits down on the curb by my feet.

"Been back to Kansas lately?"

Her voice brings me back from a nod. I scratch my nose and realize its Patti Mitchell.

"Jesus Patti, you fuckin' pregnant?"

"Nice hello."

"Well, I just…"

"I know."

We talk for a bit. She's been all over the United States. Different cities. Different scenes. She's tired. Just wants to stay put for a while. I light a cigarette, offer her one, and she takes it.

"Who's the dad?" I ask and point at her stomach.

Patti takes a drag on the cigarette and glares at the skinheads across the street. A really loud baldy breaks from the group, an alpha male goose-stepping around in his red twenty eyehole Doc Martins with the white laces. His arm poised rigid in the air Sieg Heiling, he glances over to make sure she's watching.

"Hitler youth over there your boyfriend?"

"Bash is a good guy." Patti crushes the half-smoked cigarette into the pavement. "At least, when we're alone he is."

"His fuckin' name is Bash?"

"His real name's Bob. He's a Mormon, from one of those, ah, what do you call it, where they got all those wives?"

"A polygamous sect?"

"Yeah, that's it. Bash got kicked out. The head guy wanted all the women for himself."

"Your boyfriend's a Mormon skinhead?"

"Technically, he's excommunicated. So no, he ain't Mormon no more."

A dusty four door Chevy drives past and honks. Someone in the Chevy yells. The skinheads respond throwing beer bottles, cracking the windshield. The car screeches to a stop. Four Latinos get out. The skinheads run towards them, shouting.

"I think your boyfriend just scored a touchdown."

"Fuck. He just got outta jail."

Patti runs into the ensuing melee of cholos and skinheads. She's so small I worry about her being hurt. But I'm not getting in the middle of that insanity. She grabs Bash by the hand and drags him in my direction.

"Bash, this is Patrick. An old friend."

"Dude," says Bash, and holds out his hand.

I don't want to shake Bash's hand. I don't like to come in contact with skinheads unless it's at the end of a baseball bat and I'm smacking them in the head. Then again, Bash is a Mormon. How many chances do I have of meeting a Mormon skinhead?

"Wanna bump?" Bash pulls out a baggie of dirty-looking white powder, which I'm sure is biker crank.

"No thanks."

Bash and Patti snort small piles of nasty shit off the backs of their hands. Just the idea of snorting speed is ruining my high.

"I gotta be getting back to the band. I can get you two on the guest list."

"Bash is banned from all the clubs in Houston," says Patti.

"Fuck yeah," says Bash.

The club is hot and there's no air. A bunch of kids are crowded up in front by the stage and a pathetic mosh pit has formed with less than a dozen people. Flipper is playing and Will's at the mic screaming, "Life is the only thing worth living for."

I'm thinking of that kid inside of Patti and it makes me shudder.

***

El Paso, Texas. Flipper's playing another all-ages show. The venue's an alternative warehouse space, the turnout small, but the kids are enthusiastic. Near the end of the set, Ted abruptly turns off his amp and walks off stage as the audience screams for more. I pick up the guitar, turn the amp back on, and try and play a song with the band. But I'm not Ted, it sounds like shit, and after five minutes we quit.

Everyone's tired. We're getting on each other's nerves. Even though DeMartis replaced Bruce, everyone's still in fear the tour will fall apart. The southern bookings haven't been going well. We've fewer shows and the crowds and guarantees have been smaller, leaving us with less cash, longer drives, and more downtime between shows. We didn't even have this gig in El Paso until I booked it a few weeks ago.

While the band is backstage, I find the promoter, Ed Ivey (bass: Rhythm Pigs, Black Kali Ma, Gary Floyd Band), and get our money. I know Ed from the Kennedy tours, so I take a chance and ask if he knows where to score drugs. He says he can get some weed.

"Looking for something a little stronger. Real drugs."

"A friend of mine's mom has Valiums."

It's late afternoon and everyone is hanging out in the common room of our two-bedroom suite on the fifth floor of a semi high-rise hotel in downtown El Paso. All the surrounding buildings are lower, so we have an unobstructed view of the traffic caught at the Mexican border a few blocks away. Below the hotel, there's a menudo restaurant, and even from up here, the smell of the cooking grease and spices wafting in through the open window is intense.

Everyone's a bit down, as we've just received word our next show has been canceled for lack of presales and we have the night off. Actually, without the show we have almost four days off, which isn't good. Our last few gigs haven't been very profitable. Now, we have nothing until we get to L.A.

We're all sitting around having a band meeting but it's not really that formal. I'm hoping we can get this over with so Will and I can figure out where to score dope. But, Ted has some sort of an agenda he wants to address. It's also apparent that DePace is angry about something other than the show being canceled. So, I'm listening.

"There's a show tomorrow night in San Francisco we should headline," says Ted. "I want you to call Ness at the Mab and get us on the bill. Tell him we'll do it if he pays our airfare and a thousand bucks."

I'm not really sure how to respond and take a second to think Ted's plan through. I'm a little stunned from being blindsided by such an odd demand, and more than a little annoyed by his attitude. Plus, I'm not really sure why Ted and Steve are so angry and I wonder if it's directed at me. Unfortunately, the reality is Ted's plan can't work for numerous reasons:

1. Airfare to San Francisco for four, booked at the last minute, is more money than Flipper makes even at normal out-of-town shows, but it's also more than they'd make if they played the Mab,

because it's local. So, if anything, and on the odd chance this could actually happen, the thousand bucks is definitely out of the question.

2. Ness Aquino, the Mabuhay Gardens' owner, isn't going to put up the money to fly anybody in for a show, especially not Flipper.

3. The show already has a headliner, a band Ted thinks Flipper should be playing with—but not opening for—which presents another whole set of problems trying to get them on the bill.

4. This plan leaves me hanging with the truck in Texas and having to drive to L.A. by myself, which I'd be okay with if Ted's plan actually was a halfway reasonably intelligent plan and the band was able to make some money and rejoin me in Los Angeles for the two shows that we do have there. But as it is, if they played the show for airfare, they'd be stuck in S.F., we'd have to cancel, and I'd still need to get the truck and gear back to San Francisco.

I'm looking to the other guys for support. They're avoiding eye contact and keeping their mouths shut.

"I don't think this is a good idea."

"Do your fuckin' job," yells Ted. "I'm tired of paying you to be Will's babysitter."

"Fuck you. I'm not calling Ness."

"You work for me. I fuckin' pay you. Make the call!" Ted leans across the table and jabs his finger towards me.

I flick my lit cigarette and nail him in the middle of his chest. His raggedy black sweater, a mass of sparks, starts burning, and he swats it out. Then we're both up, toe to toe, about to trade blows.

"Is this really what you all want? Because it's fuckin' stupid. Ness won't go for it."

Bruno gets between us and says to chill out. He tells me I should just make the call, see what I can work out, no harm in asking. I tell them all to go fuck themselves and storm out of the suite, slamming the door. In the hallway, I immediately regret losing my cool. I'm angry and hurt. Fuck them, the ungrateful bastards.

I have nothing against Ted. He's definitely crazy, in that good, creative, eccentric kind of way, and I like the guy. But the babysitter comment had gotten to me. Just because the tour has gotten fucked up doesn't mean I'm supposed to jump at any lame-ass idea and try and salvage what's already falling apart. I'm not the booking agent. I didn't put the tour together. I'm just the road manager. I already booked yesterday's show and, as shitty as it was, we still made money and none of them even thanked me.

I'm outside the hotel smoking a cigarette, pacing the sidewalk, pissed off, when Will and Bruno come out to find me.

"I was so close to fucking him up," I say, and kick the side of the building with my steel toed boots.

"Ted woulda killed you," says Bruno.

"I know."

I don't want to argue, or continue being angry, and I decide to let it go.

An hour later, we're all bored and restless, smoking cigarettes, talking about doing something, but none of us knows what.

"Let's go to Mexico," says Will.

We hail a passing taxi and tell the driver to take us to Juárez. He wants to know where we want to go in Juárez. I tell him we're looking for a bar or a club to hang out and drink. Will says it'd be cool if the bar has live music. The driver asks if we want any women. I tell him no. He says he knows where to go, and we'll love the women there. I say that's all right, just a bar with music will do.

The streets are dark until we hit the border and cross the bridge, then the lights are blinding. On the Mexican side, a guy in uniform asks what we're doing and where we're going.

"Tourists," our driver tells him, and we get unenthusiastically waved through.

As the glare of the border fades, we come off the bridge, cross a large, broad interchange, and turn down a street lined with brightly lit souvenir shops and tax-free liquor stores. All the buildings are painted brilliant colors and the sidewalks are crowded with people. Groups of young men standing around smoking cigarettes in front of neon-lit bars hostilely stare as we pass. Outdoor food stalls periodically line both sides of the street and there's the smell of grilled meat in the air.

The business district abruptly ends and we drive into a dark, badly lit residential neighborhood of low houses and vacant lots. The road immediately becomes rougher to drive on, and the farther we go, the worse it gets. Soon, it turns into dirt with huge potholes, the streetlights now all but absent, or they aren't working, and every thirty feet a dead dog carcass. Most of the houses have tall fences or walls around them with a dim light at the gate. Otherwise, the streets are dark, deserted, and there's no one anywhere.

The driver makes a turn onto an even worse road, with deeper potholes, and somehow another dead dog, and stops in front of a plain white house with no fence and a bright bare light bulb above the door.

"What's this?" asks Will.

"It's a club," says the driver. "Pay me. I wait for you here."

I hand him money and we all get out.

The street is pitch black. I can barely see where I'm stepping. There's no traffic, only a few parked cars that look abandoned. On my left is a huge pothole filled with brackish water. In front of me is the dead dog, illuminated in the glare of the porch light, its crushed head framed in a pool of dusty, coagulated blood.

Music is coming from inside the house. I knock on the front door. A fat, sweaty guy with greasy hair and a full Fu Manchu mustache slightly cracks open the door, checks us out, then opens it all the way and invites us inside. I walk into a front room that is so dark I have to wait for my eyes to adjust from the glare of the porch light. Dim shafts of smoke-filled light spill in from the various doorways to other rooms, but the main room doesn't appear to have any light of its own. In the center there's a jukebox, a few tables, some chairs, and a sofa. Off to the side is a pool table, and in the next room there's a bare mattress on the floor.

Two girls dressed in see-through negligées and panties pretend to be playing a game of pool. They eye us, touch themselves, and giggle. One of them bends over the table as if making a shot. She's barefoot, her large stomach hangs onto the green felt, and her ass wiggles as she moves. The other girl runs her hand up and down the pool cue in an obvious and suggestive manner. They are possibly two of the most unattractive women I have ever seen.

A man approaches from out of the dark and asks what we want.

"Cervezas," says Bruno.

I'm glad someone remembers Spanish.

We stand in the middle of the room and wait for the beers. In the dark corners, doorways, and alcoves, shifty-looking dudes check us out. A curvaceous woman wearing only a sleeveless undershirt that's straining to contain her ample body, smiles and gestures to a grungy couch, and we all sit down. The floor is littered with cigarette butts and empty beer cans. I notice that she, too, is barefoot and immediately think of tetanus. When she walks away, I watch her naked butt checks rumble and sway.

The beers arrive, they're bottled, not cans. Sadly, it's American beer, and because of this the man wants a ridiculous sum for money. We pay him, not knowing what else to do. The tune on the jukebox ends and the room goes silent, the clack of pool balls the only sound.

No one is saying anything. It's like they're waiting for us to do something and we're not doing anything but drinking beer. Obviously, this is a whorehouse and we're supposed to be here to check out the women. Yet, the whole situation is uncomfortable, and there's a menacing air about the place. The shifty looking dudes stare at us as if we're doing a great injustice just being here. But if it is indeed a whorehouse, then they want customers, right? So is it our appearance they don't like?

Yet, being the dope fiend that I am, I'm trying to figure out if there's any way to get drugs. But everybody's expression says they want to kill me or maybe just rip me off. I'm afraid to further crank up the hostility by asking about heroin. It's like I'm the prey and they're the predators and anything I do to push the power balance their way will get me killed. I'm not that confident if I do score that any one of these dudes, or our cab driver, won't sell us out to the federales. The idea of spending time in the Juárez jail is enough of an incentive for me to simply drink my beer and keep quiet.

Fifteen minutes of the girls in the corner giggling and the scary dudes staring with dead eyes, and I've had enough.

"I'm outta here." I put down my empty beer and walk to the door. A guy dressed in black, wearing a cowboy hat, steps off a stool and partially blocks my way. I say excuse me, move around him, and go outside. The air feels cool after being in that airless house. The cab is gone. The street is desolate and deserted except for the dead dog, which is still there and still quite dead.

The rest of the band gradually files out behind me. We look at each other, but no one says anything. After a minute or two, our cab turns the corner and slowly creeps toward us. We all get in and ride back to the hotel in silence.

* * *

Long Beach, California, Fender's Ballroom. We're playing an exclusive one-L.A.-show-only gig. Except, Ted's girlfriend Sheri has booked another show the next night in Hollywood with Fishbone. It should be a good show, although I don't know the promoters and distrust Sheri's ability to not get taken by them. But the real problem is if Fender's finds out we've reneged on the "exclusive clause" of the contract then they could renege on our guarantee. Which having sold out, Fender's is going to be quite sizable and will make up for the last couple of dismal shows.

I'm at the door to the box office talking to the club manager and the ticket seller. Through the glass front I see Mike Roche and Ron Emory from T.S.O.L. and tell the ticket seller that they're on our guest list and to let them in. "I would've let them in anyway," she says. I guess being local rock stars does have its advantages.

Over their shoulders, I see Sheri passing out flyers and my stomach turns. "Excuse me," I say and rush outside and grab Sheri. "What the fuck are you doing?"

"I'm promoting my show. Maybe if you did stuff like this the tour wouldn't have sucked so bad!"

"You can't do that here."

"Why the fuck not?"

"We've signed a contract for only one L.A. show."

"No one told me."

I know I've told her, and I told Ted. I specifically said we shouldn't even mention the Hollywood show to anyone until we're off the stage and paid at Fender's, and Sheri had said, "But how will I promote it?"

"That's your problem. I didn't even okay this show in the first place."

"You're not their manager."

"Neither are you!"

Ten years later, Sheri and I will run into each other. She'll be married with a kid. I'll be back at Mission A shooting speed, trying to stay off heroin. We initially start using together. Then, we eventually start fucking, which is the nature of speed. Your senses are on overload and the sex part comes out nowhere. Speed freaks will fuck anything that moves and some things that don't. Desires are amped up to pervert level, and sex becomes the fantasy of sweaty porn.

Sheri and her husband and kid move to Sacramento, we'll lose touch. Then out of nowhere she'll resurface. I burn a friend of hers, shorting them on a speed deal. I'm back on heroin, living with Gina, and I don't really care.

When I get out of prison in 2000, I'm in rehab and Sheri finds me again. We talk on the phone. I tell her I'm off dope, living in a rehab, and I'm in recovery. She says she's clean too. We make plans to get together. The next night she calls again. She's drunk and accuses me of not loving her. I don't know what to say. I hang up the phone.

Ten years later, I get a text from Jimmy Crucifix (guitar: Crucifix, The Next, Proud Flesh) that Sheri is in the hospital. "It's not looking promising. She stopped breathing and her heart stopped, and it took forty-five minutes to revive her. She was without oxygen for forty-five minutes... Was so sad to see her in that condition. So lifeless!"

And then, the next day, I'm in a parking lot outside an NA meeting and my phone chimes: "Results of the brain scan came in... Sheri's gone forever... "

I tell Sheri to knock off handing out flyers and then walk around the parking lot smoking a cigarette trying to cool down. This is fucking crazy and so typically Flipper. That they'd risk fucking up a decent guarantee is just business as usual. I'm stoked that the tour is almost over and I'll be free of these guys.

The truck is parked at the side of the building, and I walk over to sit inside and avoid everyone. Will is talking to a skinny guy, obviously doing a drug deal.

"You'll be back before the end of the show, right Mike? We gotta leave right after."

The skinny guy says of course he will and I'm thinking Will is nuts.

"You want in on this?"

"No thanks."

Never give your money to a junkie and then tell them you're leaving town. But more than anything, don't give your money to a junkie without getting the dope at the same time.

"That guy's not coming back, Will."

"Yeah, he is. That's Mike Ness from Social Distortion. He's a friend."

The manager is waiting for me. "What the fuck is this?!" He screams, thrusting Sheri's flyer in my face. I do my best to act surprised. "I have no fucking idea."

"Do you know what 'exclusive' means?"

"Yes, I do."

"You just broke our agreement."

This is all really just bullshit posturing on the manager's part. The venue is sold out. He couldn't have done any better than that. Except, now he sees an opportunity to pay us less and I can't fault him. I told Ted and Sheri that this was a definite probability if they booked another date and they ignored me.

After the show, I get paid a lot less than I should and even though I argue with the manager my heart just isn't into it. I'm hoping we'll make it up at tomorrow's show in Hollywood. But, really, the tour is over and it's time to go home.

As Ted starts up the truck, Will stands out in the empty parking lot acting all forlorn like he's waiting for his lost dog to come home.

"I gotta wait for Mike."

"He's not coming." I pull Will into the truck.

Two years later, I'll be living in the Bronx in New York City, my life having fallen apart and I'm no longer touring. I'll be out there trying to stay off heroin but drinking myself to death. Late one night close to Christmas, I'll get the phone call that Will OD'ed, and I'll be devastated. Will and I had gotten really close. His relationship with Brenda had ended, he was living with another woman, they were expecting their first child, and his drug use had been considerably curtailed. From the outside at least, it appeared he'd gotten his life somewhat together. The night before I left S.F., I'd made a pact with Will that we'd stop shooting dope. Neither of us was able to keep that promise.

SHE LOST CONTROL
1985: SAN FRANCISCO

Even the street dealers are pissed at Anna Lisa. She owes everyone money. A dealer I don't even know threatens me at knifepoint in front of Mission A. The situation has gone from bad to fucking deplorable and it's become more than glaringly obvious I can't leave Anna Lisa on her own anymore.

A short East Coast Kennedys tour is coming up. We need someone to sell T-shirts. I tell Microwave I'm hiring Anna Lisa. He asks if I'm sure, because it's a bad idea. Everyone involved tells me not to bring my girlfriend on the road. It's like an unwritten rule—a rule I've actually enforced. But I'm so secretive about my drug habit that nobody really knows my situation. I'm not worried about the usual things that others worry about, like Anna Lisa running into any women I've fucked. I'm more stressed on how I'm going to keep both of us well. Scoring drugs on the road can be challenging. Although if there's one thing Anna Lisa excels at, it is finding drugs, so I really needn't worry. If I leave her here, it's just going to get worse. She's depressed and suicidal. I am scared she won't be alive when I come back.

Two years later, Anna Lisa and I will have been kicked out of Mission A for selling heroin and too many people overdosing, including myself. We'll be living in an apartment above S.F. General Hospital on Potrero Hill owned by my stepfather. Anna Lisa will have gotten approved for SSI (Supplemental Security Income), a federal income program for the disabled. It's another junkie scam. A doctor diagnosed her for severe depression. In reality, she's not faking and her depression is really bad. Between SSI and my family, we've become dependent on others to take care of us. Our existence will be Anna Lisa's monthly checks, my paltry income working for Alternative Tentacles, the odd painting job my stepfather throws my way, my mother helping out with the rent, and whatever drug deals we can put together.

At Mission A our addiction had already been way out of control. Now it was all-consuming and our lives were even more of a horrible mess. If we're not loaded, we're in bed kicking. There are days and weeks we never leave the apartment. Anna Lisa becomes sullen and withdrawn. More often than not, she's taken a handful of pills and is in bed asleep. I should've been more attentive, seen the warning signs that Anna Lisa was spiraling into a deep depression. But being the good self-absorbed addict that I was, I didn't.

On Halloween Eve, despondent over the anniversary of her mother committing suicide jumping in front of a BART train, Anna Lisa will attempt to kill herself. She'll ingest copious amounts of alcohol, a full prescription of Xanax, numerous shots of heroin, and a plethora of other drugs that I had no idea she was hoarding. When the reality sets in that she's actually going to die, she calls my mother who picks her up and takes her to the nearby hospital. On the drive there, Anna Lisa will tell my mother we're junkies. This not only blows my life totally apart, but also sends me into damage control. I tell my family I'm ready to quit and agree to relocate to my sister's on the East Coast to dry out. Anna Lisa enters a thirty-day rehab. We're never really together again.

AT MY JOB
1985: DEAD KENNEDYS

Microwave is busy running Alternative Tentacles for Biafra and he's retiring from touring. With the natural progression of promoting from within the crew, I'm set to be the next road manager. Only, Biafra says no. He wants a high profile/politically correct person in the slot. He again taps Kris Carleson from Ken Lester's Crisis Management. I'm totally pissed off. I feel I've put in the work and now it's my time. I road manage other bands. Why not the Kennedys? It sucks Biafra has no faith in me. My feelings get hurt. I let it go. Only I make it clear Carleson may be the road manager, but I'm head of the road crew.

I hire Chris Grayson as soundman and Anna Lisa and Candace Batycki (from Canada) to sell T-shirts. Now, the only problem is finding a roadie. I know a bunch of dudes who fit the bill. Except, everyone seems to be out on tour or have scheduling conflicts. What I'm really looking for is someone to deal with all the jocks and skinheads. After three years of getting into fights, I'm tired and don't want to be the only man on stage against the world. After a lot of discussion, Microwave and I decide to hire Ron Shasberg, the kick boxer from Holland.

What a roadie does: roadies do all the
grunt work. They lift the heavy gear,
set up the stage, keep the instruments

tuned, and save the band's ass when shit goes bad. Roadies make sure the set list, beer, water, and towels are on stage and everything is ready before the band emerges to the screams of their adoring audience. Roadies keep the stagedivers off the gear, the mic stands aloft, and the drum kit tight and running. Roadies tackle the occasional overzealous fan who feels the need to grope the lead singer, and if there's any violence, they make sure it ends before it gets started. Roadies break the gear down, load-out after the show, and drive all night to the next venue. They stay two to a room in seedy motels, live off all-night diner food, and do their laundry on the odd day off in a forlorn launderette in the bad part of some nameless city. Roadies are, for the most part, unrequited musicians, some with their own bands, and they get almost no recognition for all the hard work they do.

We're all set to fly out to the East Coast. We're picking up a bobtail truck from Hertz and renting gear from SRI. All our flights are booked on People Express—a new airline that's so low budget you have to practically load the luggage onto the plane yourself. I have Ray's guitars in a large road case and Klaus's bass safely stored in a flight case. I'm hoping this cheap-ass airline doesn't lose them.

The crew and the entire band, except Biafra, take the same flight to Newark. This will become the normal procedure for Dead

Kennedys as Ray and Biafra start drifting more and more apart. Kris Carleson's job will also entail being a personal assistant to Biafra. I'm reminded of Ted Falconi's anger towards me when "babysitting" Will Shatter for Flipper was part of my job description. I make a mental note to give Carleson a break. If she's dealing with Biafra and making him happy, then my job is easier.

What a road manager does: road mangers get handed a tour itinerary and groan at the logistical nightmare the booker has bestowed upon them. Road managers secure the vehicle rentals, plane tickets, hotel rooms, and any other travel arrangements the band requires (and there is always some pain-in-the-ass problem with flights and hotels). Road managers ride with the crew and call ahead to the venues and get all the technical issues worked out. Road managers deal with journalists, TV, and radio, setting up interviews. Road managers keep tabs on the merchandise, make sure there are enough T-shirts, and the printers are sending more. Road managers keep the road crew happy, they placate the band members, and ease whatever concerns the promoter might have when the band arrives and acts like prima donna assholes. Road mangers insist the band's rider is fulfilled and the promoter provides everything that's been agreed on. Road managers

round up the band and get them ready
to go on stage. Road mangers clear the
backstage dressing room of all the
hangers-on and most importantly get
paid at the end of the night. Road
mangers take a lot of shit from the
band, road crew, and promoters. They
get all the credit for a successful tour
and all the blame for a bad one.

I have a quarter ounce of heroin for the road. Or I should say
Anna Lisa is holding our quarter ounce of heroin as she has major
trust issues. We're at the gate and airport security is X-raying our
bags. I'm already through, picking up my bag, and watching the X-
ray monitor as Anna Lisa's passes under it. In amongst all the vague,
shaded areas of clothes and shoes there's a clear outline of a spoon
and several syringes she's stashed in an old cigarette case. The
security person either doesn't realize what she's looking at, or
doesn't care, and passes the bag through.

The plane is a huge Boeing 747 with a row of seats in the
middle of the cabin that Chris, Candace, Anna Lisa, and I are sitting
in. After takeoff, we take turns shooting up in bathroom. Anna Lisa
and I go in together to shoot up but also fuck. When we come out,
people smile at us. For the rest of the flight, we're nodding out,
comatose.

We touch down and it's a nightmare trying to find our
luggage and the guitars. Ray and Klaus have hotels booked in
Manhattan and they take off. D.H. is staying with the crew at our
motel in New Jersey. Of all the Kennedys, he's the only one who
actually kicks it with the road crew.

We finally locate the guitars and luggage; they got pulled for
being "oversized," which is airline talk for losing the bags and then
finding them in a place they weren't supposed to be. Now we're out

at the curb trying to get a cab. People Express is located in a terminal that only stays open when People Express is flying, and we came in on their last flight. A skycap tells me he'll try and get us transportation and disappears.

D.H. is wandering around looking for something to eat. "I'm fucking starving." Everything in the terminal is closed. He says, "I'll be right back." I tell him not to go far; we're waiting on a cab.

"Don't worry, man." D.H. walks off in the direction of another terminal.

An hour later, a shuttle van pulls up and honks. The van is a wreck. It's dented and scratched up and the front bumper is held on with bungee cords. I can barely make out the company logo on the passenger door. The driver, a skinny man with a heavy Bronx accent, says the skycap called and he's here to pick us up. When I tell him where we're going, he shakes his head in disgust and says it's a hundred bucks to drive the six miles to our motel. I'm figuring this is either totally legit or we're going get killed, our bodies left by the side of the road, and the luggage and gear stolen. Since the terminal closed, there hasn't been any traffic. I really don't have a choice.

"We're the fuck is D.H.?"

The driver is impatient. He's telling me it's either now or never. Candace and Anna Lisa are bitching, wanting to go to the motel. Chris shrugs his shoulders. "Your call."

"Fuck."

We pack all the gear into the van. I tell the driver to wait fifteen more minutes. I'll pay him twenty-five dollars more.

"It's your dime," he says.

After fifteen minutes and no D.H., the driver says he's leaving. Get the gear out, or let's go. We all pile in the van and take off.

"Fuck."

The motel is a sleazy fleabag in an industrial section of Elizabeth, New Jersey. We've booked two rooms, it's 4 PM, and neither of them is ready. We stack all our bags and gear by the manager's office and wait. A parade of crackheads and junkies stumble in and out of the parking lot. A couple of shifty-looking dudes hang outside their room drinking from paper cups and eyeing us hard. There's absolutely nothing on the same street as the motel, no restaurant, no corner store... nothing. All of us haven't eaten since this morning and we're hungry.

I walk around the block looking for a restaurant or at least a liquor store. Across the highway is an Exxon station with a Circle K. We can at least buy snacks if nothing else pans out.

Circle K "convenience" stores are the bastard children to 7-Eleven's and all other mini-marts. They are almost always located on the worst side of town or way out in the boonies off some desolate highway exit. When we're on the road and in a hurry, this is where we stop to eat while filling up with gas. They don't have Slurpies or Big Gulps, and their products are more generic with fewer frills. Their red-hot beef and bean burritos go completely nuclear in the microwave. When you rip open the plastic sheath you have to wait until they cool, or the first bite adheres to the roof of your mouth like molten lava. The coffee is 60 weight crude oil. There's always a dozen hotdogs spinning on a rolling "grill" and the entire store reeks of rancid oil. The smoldering vat of "nacho cheese" could probably do double duty as filler to patch holes in a wall. I don't know why but we always seem to end up at a Circle K. But I wouldn't have it any other way.

A surly maid rolls her cart out of the back of the motel. She glares at us as she opens the doors to our rooms. Twenty minutes later we're inside, lying on the beds and smoking. The rooms are adjoining with one of those creepy doors you can open between them. I hate having a door to another room when I don't know who is in the next room. It's just weird. Now it's kind of cool.

I'm worried about D.H. but what can I do? I call Microwave and tell him what's up, and he laughs, "You lost D.H.?" This doesn't placate my fears and, in fact, Micro laughing at me just makes them worse. I have no idea how to get ahold of D.H. or where he would go. I don't even know what hotel Ray and Klaus are staying at. Microwave booked our motel, and I'm hoping D.H. calls Micro and gets the address or at least the phone number. I don't even know where Carleson and Biafra are, as she never told us or gave me anyone's travel itinerary.

The motel comes alive after dark. Hookers line the street out front, and the johns are cruising. Half the cars in the motel parking lot are here for twenty minutes. There's a quick turnover. Chris and I walk to the Circle K and pick up beer and cigarettes. A gang of young thugs huddles along the side of the building and scope us out. "You looking?" they ask. What else would a couple of white boys be doing in this neighborhood at night but scoring drugs?

"No thanks, man."

An undercover cop car screeches to a halt. Two plain-clothes cops burst out the doors and charge toward the group of thugs. A bottle gets thrown, there's shouting, a scuffle turns into a full-blown fight, and another patrol car flies up with siren and lights on. There are gunshots and everyone hits the pavement.

Trying our best to look inconspicuous, we cautiously walk through the ensuing anarchy at the Circle K parking lot. Carrying our bag of snacks and beer, we make our way to the relative safety across the highway as more cop cars flood the scene. In the distance, a refinery billows out dark smoke. The entire town smells like diesel fuel. A hooker asks if I want a date. Feeling awkward, I mumble no. "It's okay, white boy. You can talk to me. I don't bite... unless you want me to."

***

Lupo's Heartbreak Hotel, Providence, Rhode Island. The opening bands have played. We're set up. The Kennedys are ready to go on. The only problem is there's no D.H. I explained to the band what happened at the airport. No one has heard from him since.

Ray and Klaus are standing by their amps, instruments in hand. Biafra takes the mic. "We're missing our drummer. We can either not play, or try out a couple of volunteer drummers from the opening bands..."

The crowd screams for them to play. A drummer from one of the opening acts says he can play all the D.K. songs. There's another guy from a band that didn't play who claims he can too. Suddenly, more "drummers" are rushing forward. We're trying to decide which one to try first when there's a commotion at the front door. D.H. pushes through the crowd, jumps up on stage, and gets behind the drum kit.

"You all right?" I yell.

D.H. flips me off with both hands and screams, "Fuck you, man. Fuck you!" Then the entire crowd takes up the chant. They're all flipping me off and screaming fuck you. The band breaks into "Police Truck." D.H. is playing his drums so hard they're literally falling apart. I'm trying to upright his floor tom when he nails me in the hand with his drumstick.

***

The Showplace is a dump. What else would you expect from a strip club in Dover, New Jersey that transforms itself into a music venue when touring bands come though? I've been here with T.S.O.L. so I know what to expect. Yet, the forlorn interior and the dank stench of stale beer and cigarettes hits hard as I walk in the door.

We're early loading in for soundcheck and the strippers are still on stage: sad-looking middle-aged women, meth-head biker mamas, showing cellulite, wrinkles, and stretch marks. Their old man is probably sitting in the dark somewhere in the audience, or at the bar, nursing a beer and a grudge. The same guys who are going to work the front door, be bouncers, and back me up as security. We show up in our leather jackets, motorcycle boots, torn Levi's, and black cut-off T-shirts—and all of them are in roughly the same uniform, although in sizes a lot larger.

I step up to the bar, order a beer, and light a cigarette. The bartender tells me I can't run a tab.

"I just want a fucking beer." I hand her a twenty. She stares at me like I'm the worst scum she's ever seen. A pretty hard feat to achieve in a club like The Showplace. When she gives me change, I tip her a dollar and her expression softens.

Dude on the stool next to me is glaring at the half-naked woman hanging off a pole on the stage behind the bar. He's a big-ass motherfucker with a mane of greasy black hair, an arm full of faded blue tats, and a leather vest with some obscure bike gang colors on the back. I drink my beer and watch the stripper spread her legs, straddle the pole, and grind into the phallic brass erection, her pink rhinestone g-string shimmering in the stage lights. Her breasts poke straight up and out, perky, perfect—a boob job on an aging body.

"Don't look at her," says the biker.

"Excuse me?"

"That's my wife, don't look at her."

"This place is fucking unreal," I say to Chris.

We're backstage. The show's started. It's packed. Not much happens in Dover, and a Dead Kennedys show draws every punk kid in a fifty-mile radius. We also bring in the occasional adventurists, angry nonconformists, skinheads, local weirdos, wannabe hipsters, and the usual assortment of the lost and disenfranchised.

"Unreal as in a slice of existence that's trapped in a surreal time warp unreal?"

"Ah, yeah. Something like that… you take acid again?"

"The Showplace never changes," says Chris, ignoring my question. "If it did, my lack of faith in humanity would too."

We're both tired. Sleep hasn't been a priority. Touring the East Coast is easier. States are smaller. Venues closer. Drives shorter. But that still never seems to help.

The second band, Junk Yard, is a bunch of kids from Washington, D.C. and D.H. got them on the bill. Other than Bad Brains and Fishbone, Black punk bands playing shows outside of major cities are still a bit of a rarity, and D.H. is doing whatever he can to change that.

Over the years that I've known and worked with D.H., the punk scene has continued to be predominately white. With the rise of skinheads and hardcore, it had only gotten worse. On tour, we'd be in these small-town venues where racism was the norm, upfront, and in-your-face. All the bands were white. The audience was white. The venues were white. The cops that shut us down were white. All those shows with D.H. being the only Black man in the entire place, I'd have to have been unconscious not to feel his sense of isolation. I can't help but think D.H. being so goddamn angry for me leaving him at the Trenton airport when he up and disappeared has more to do with continually feeling disrespected. In his mind, what happened was just another example, but this time from someone he trusted. This made it worse, and he's directing all that pent-up anger and frustration at me.

But then neither of us really talks about it.

By the time the Kennedys hit the stage, The Showplace is so full it's about to burst. We're halfway through the set and it's pure insanity. There's no air, it's hot as hell, and the crowd is pressing against the front of the stage. I'm on Klaus's side, behind me there's a six-foot drop onto the passageway to backstage. There's no rail, just the monitor board and cases of beer stacked along the wall. All the biker security dudes are there, watching the show, talking shit, and drinking.

I toss a couple of stagedivers into the crowd. There's no fucking room and I'm conscious of falling off. I keep in close, behind the amps. A first-class nutjob makes his way onto my side of the stage. He's screaming at the top of his lungs, doing an Al Pacino tough guy routine. In his hand is a folding knife that he flicks open and then closes. I gesture to the closest biker and point to the guy. He just shrugs. Pacino dude is obviously crazy and these motherfuckers don't want to deal with him. They'll probably just let him walk on stage.

It's between songs and Biafra is talking his usual banter to the crowd. He's yelling, but this crazy Pacino dude is standing by the side-fills yelling louder and he doesn't even have a mic. I'd really like to get him off stage, but I'm not too happy about Pacino dude's knife. I've been stabbed before, that shit hurts, and I'm gun shy.

Fed up with competing, Biafra charges crazy Pacino dude and shoves him backward off the stage down into the passageway. Crazy Pacino dude doesn't even see it coming and seriously takes a fall six feet down and hits the cement floor hard with a thud. Then he's up and screaming revenge. The bikers grab him and twist his arms behind his back and hustle him out the side door.

The band starts the next song with most of the crowd unaware of what happened. The huge biker from earlier at the bar comes up and leans in, "Careful loading out. That 'lil guy's fuckin' pissed. Gonna be gunnin' for you'se throwing 'em off stage."

"Can't you guys just beat the shit outta him so I don't gotta deal with it?"

"They don't pays me enough to mess with fuckwads like dat."

They don't pay me enough either, I'm thinking.

Biafra's in the audience, held up above the crowd, kneeling on shoulders, with his back to the stage. He's arched upward, under a glaring white stage light, the mic held above his head as he screams the encore's chorus:

"C'mon bleed
C'mon bleed
C'mon bleed
Bleed for me"

A spray of blood red liquid splatters Biafra, dousing the ceiling and those around him. A teenage girl screams. Her hands touch her face. She's cover in red liquid. There's panic and pandemonium, the crowd parts, and everyone around Biafra is drenched. I watch him go down and think someone has finally killed him. That fucking crazy Pacino dude stabbed Biafra. He's fucking dead.

I glance over at Klaus. He's staring wide-eyed but hasn't stopped playing. We're probably both thinking the same thing. I leap into the crowd to find out what the fuck is going on. Biafra is making his way to the stage. He's shirtless and covered in thick red liquid that eerily resembles blood. I ask if he's all right. He looks stunned and ignores me. Then I remember he's not wearing his contacts and can't see a thing. But I don't see any obvious wounds. So I follow him through the crowd and get him back up on stage.

A woman who works in a hospital, or maybe it was a friend of hers who works as a nurse, brought a plastic blood transfusion bag to the show waiting for the right moment to present itself—the ultimate punk act—to spray Biafra with blood while he sings "Bleed for Me."

The show is over. Crazy Pacino dude isn't around. When he became so out of control he tried stabbing the bikers in front of the club, they finally perceived him as a threat and six of them took turns stomping him into the ground. Although now they'd heard about Biafra getting doused with blood, they're all grumbling about missing the *real* show.

Giant biker dude finds me on stage packing up the gear. Tells me not to worry. "Took care dat guy," he says.

I want to say, "Why didn't you do that right from the

beginning?" Instead, I decide to just be grateful I'm not dealing with that crazy fucker by myself out in the dark parking lot.

***

New York City. The Algonquin Hotel. I shoot two bags of dope, get the warm rush, a weird chemical taste, a bit of itchiness, and then it's gone.

"Fuck!" I toss the rig across the room. "Did we get burned? I don't feel shit."

"Nah. I feel it." Chris scratches the bridge of his nose and leans down in that universal "junkie-on-the-nod" posture. "Yeah, it's good."

Anna Lisa ties off her arm with this intense look of concentration on her face, the tip of her tongue sticking out the side of her mouth like a kid. "White dope… they cut it… shit that's not heroin. I don't trust it. Or… you got a bad bag. Just do more."

We had hit New York a day early and checked into the hotel. Anna Lisa and I immediately took a taxi to the Lower East Side and went shopping. Within twenty minutes, we scored three bundles of ten tightly folded glassine bags, their brand names stamped on the sides. We bought 357 from a sniveling dope fiend on Avenue A, right as we got out of the cab. Two blocks later a cool Puerto Rican kid sporting a Che T-shirt, porkpie hat, and heavy gold chains sold us Red Star. "This shit is tight, yo." Anna Lisa, feeling homesick, asked a local junkie if she knew where there was any black tar heroin, "You know, like the dope from Mexico." The skinny woman got all excited and said, yes, they sold Mexican at a bodega off 2nd. "Hey, I helped you out. You owe me!" She screamed as we walked away. But it turned out the only "Mexican" part of that bodega's dope was the little man in a sombrero stamped on the small package.

We bought a bundle anyway and giggled like twelve-year-olds in the taxi as we rode back uptown.

After shooting weird shit in Montreal that was cut with methadone, and then making do with the small amount of overpriced, weak dope we scored last night in Syracuse, I'm finally relaxed; secure we've enough to last a few days. With an entire day free, all I want to do is sit around the hotel room, get loaded, and eat pizza. Only I shot the dope, I'm not loaded, and it's pissing me off. Chris and Anna Lisa are obviously high so the shit can't be bad. I take three bags, one from each brand, and pour them into the spoon.

The rush is intense. I'm definitely feeling it.

Something is scraping my toes and tops of my feet, like rough sandpaper scratching my skin. It's a major rug burn. I want it to stop. There's a dull light creeping into to my darkness. This black void is way too comfortable. I hear voices, far away. Someone slaps my face. It almost hurts.

I open my eyes. I'm in the hotel hallway. It's dark. The lights have been turned down low. All the walls are beige, and the trim is cream. I'm wondering what's with all the warm tones. It's too conventional. What about some color? Then I see the rug, gray stripes behind horrid red and gold floral trumpets, and realize the interior decorator was a sadist.

Chris and Ron each have an arm and are holding me upright. They're dragging me down the hallway. Every few feet Ron slaps my face. "What the fuck, Micky."

"Keep him moving. He's coming to." Chris shakes me. "You there?"

A door opens. Bright light spills into the darkness. D.H.'s silhouette is framed in the doorway. "What the...? Not looking too good, Slick."

I try to shrug, only with Chris and Ron holding me up it doesn't really work. My throat is so dry I can't swallow. My tongue feels like cardboard.

"I need a smoke."

"Jesus, man. You scared the hell out of us."

We're doing two shows back-to-back with Chris Williamson's Rock Hotel Productions. We're playing The World on 2nd Street, a massive old, decrepit venue that would later be a front-runner in New York's House scene. The first night's bill was: D.O.A., Reagan Youth, Adrenalin O.D., and Target of Demand. Tonight is Butthole Surfers, Live Skull, False Prophets, and Antidam.

Security is the glue-sniffing skinheads Williamson usually uses and, like all his shows, there's a sense that any one of them could go postal on a PCP bender in a moment's notice. I know Earl; he's Black, a skinhead, used to date a friend of Denise Ondayko's, and pretends to work for Williamson. Only, he really doesn't. It's just that security is afraid of him. He's way too volatile even for them. Instead of confronting Earl, they just let him shove his way into all the shows.

False Prophets is on stage, and Earl and I are hiding in the stairwell to the dressing room talking shit. A skinny white guy dressed all in black leather with blonde spiked hair tries to get past us. Earl gets in his face and asks for his backstage pass. The guy snarls his lip and with a thick cockney accent tells Earl to fuck off. Earl grabs him in a headlock and tosses him down the stairs.

"That was fuckin' Billy Idol." Earl laughs, sounding like a maniac, "Showed that fuckin' wanker."

Earl is now affecting a horrible British accent, one that he'll go in and out of all night. Earl's grip on reality is not too tight. I seriously doubt that was Billy Idol. But I'm not going to argue with Earl.

Backstage is ridiculously crowded. It seems like everyone has a backstage pass. There are so many people I can barely move, and I have to shove my way through the crowd.

I invited my sister, Scott, and her boyfriend, Neil, to the show. To my surprise they actually show up. Scott designs accessories for Liz Claiborne, and Neil is senior vice president of advertising and marketing for Barneys New York. I don't think they've ever been to a real punk show and definitely not one as large as this.

We're in the dressing room drinking beers when Biafra arrives. He takes one look at all the people and beelines over to me. "You have to clear this room. Who the fuck are all these people?"

Biafra wants to make a set list and do his vocal exercises, but he doesn't want to appear like a prima donna rock star. "Some of these people can definitely go." He's eyeing Scott and Neil, dressed in casual yuppie khakis and Izod shirts. They are obviously not punks and therefore fair game. "Like who are these people?"

"They're not going anywhere. This is my sister and her boyfriend."

Biafra screws up his face and gives me dead eyes. "I need quiet," he hisses and storms off carrying all his worldly possessions stuffed in a pillowcase he no doubt stole from the hotel.

I take Scott and Neil backstage to watch Butthole Surfers. Gibby Haynes is out of control. He's in the middle of the stage, lighting a solitary cymbal on fire with lighter fluid and striking it with a drumstick—the ignited gas is going everywhere—a fire marshal's nightmare. Paul Leary's guitar is so loud I'm partially deaf for the rest of the night. Their trademark strobe lights and backdrop screening of autopsy films assault my senses. I always wonder if the Butthole's strobes have ever caused any epileptics in the audience to go into a fit. When Gibby pulls out the clothespins and attaches them to his nipples and chest, my sister is thoroughly grossed out. To their credit, Scott and Neil stay all the way through the Kennedys' set as well.

We've parked the Hertz truck outside The Algonquin on 44th Street for the last four days. In the morning, it's gone. We've a 10AM load out for The World and we're on a tight schedule. There are signs up and down the street and the actual times allowed for parking are hard to decipher. Many of the signs conflict with one another. Some even outright say "no parking." But it's fucking New York and no one pays attention to shit like that. I talk with the hotel concierge and tell him our truck is gone. He gives me a number for the impound yard. "There's no reason they'd tow your truck. They haven't enforced those laws in years."

The tow yard is way the hell out in Queens. When I call, they can't give me an explanation why the truck was towed. I'm fuming mad and I scream over the phone until I get a pounding headache.

I send Chris and Ron in a taxi with a stack of cash out to Queens to get the goddamn truck. It's outright extortion, but what can I do?

The lock on the driver side is broken. The glove box and console has been rifled through. There are maps on the floor and an empty can of soda sitting on the dash that's definitely not ours. Thankfully, Chris had the foresight to lock the latch to the cargo access so no one could get in through the cab. The huge industrial paddle lock for the backdoor was still intact. No one got in that way.

I meet Ron and Chris at The World and we load out. The venue seems so forlornly seedy in the daylight. The stench of sour old booze is overpowering, and there's a murky patina of grungy dirt everywhere that you can't see when the lights are down low.

We pull into the same parking spot in front of the hotel. The uniformed doorman to the adjoining hotel runs out screaming. "You can't park that fuckin' beast here!" He's red in the face, jumping up and down, and shaking his fist at us. "Already had it towed once, I'll do it again."

Chris, Ron and I get out of the truck. "You had our truck towed?"

"I can't see the taxis down the street."

Chris grabs the doorman by the front of his shirt and slams him into the side of the truck. I put my finger in the man's face. "We're parking here and going into our hotel. If this truck isn't here when we come out, or when-ever-the-fuck for however long we're here and it's gone again, you're fuckin' dead."

Ron smacks the guy in the head for good measure.

"Okay, okay, jeez fellows. Just tryin' do my job."

"Lucky I ain't making you pay the impound fee."

I'm shaking with unrequited violence and at the same time surprised at how quick I am to anger. These days I have no problem with violence. I want to fucking hurt this guy. I have to walk away before this escalates and I actually do.

NOTHIN' FOR YOU
1985: T.S.O.L.

T.S.O.L.'s van is dying. It's safe to say it's seen better days, and, loaded down with seven guys and pulling a trailer full of gear and merchandise, isn't helping. The carburetor sputters, the van hesitates, and the engine dies. Ron is driving and does his best to pull to the side of the highway: a two-lane piece of shit running due south through Arkansas. We're taking a "shortcut" by dropping down from Interstate 40 on our way to Baton Rouge. We had thought to take the scenic route, but we've broken one of the major rules of touring—never get off the interstate.

The bullet hole-riddled road sign a few yards down says we're entering Lake Village. Ron turns the key, and the van starts and roughly idles. We jerkily drive into Lake Village. There's a gas station, a motel, a do-it-yourself car wash, and a junkyard with a small hand-painted sign that reads, "auto repair." Ron steers us into the junkyard and we get out of the van. Two Black guys in overalls look up from under the hood of a Chevy.

"Something's wrong with our van," says Mike Roche.

The Black guys stare at us, but don't say a word. It's the South. We're not sure what the local protocol is. We exchange glances while Chris walks over to talk to them.

We played in Oklahoma City last night and even though the venue was small, it was a good show and sold out. Afterward, the owner closed the club and invited us to "party." The building was a windowless bunker, and as the party progressed, we had no idea what time it was, other than it was well past 2AM. The alcohol flowed. The music was a lot of bad rap and very loud. There were unattractive local girls, and all the dudes were wannabe thugs wearing backward baseball caps with tractor company logos on them. When we finally emerged to head over to the motel to get some sleep, it was too late. The sun was already up, and we had to get on the road.

Now, broke down in Lake Village, we're hungover, bleary eyed, and awake.

The mechanics agree to drop what they're doing and fix our van. We thank them profusely and leave in search of a place to chill out. Yet, once we actually walk around Lake Village, we realize there isn't anywhere to hang out. I mean there wasn't anything at the first glance, but the second says there *really* wasn't anything. Roche remembers a motel as we drove into town. We all head back to the van, grab our bags, and walk in that direction.

The band rents a room. They're sitting around watching TV. Chris and I head back to the junkyard. The weather is muggy, the sky overcast. I keep thinking it's going to rain, but it doesn't. At a gas station mini-mart, we get a couple of beers and a half pint and walk along the side of the road drinking them out of paper bags. There doesn't seem to be a local cop. There doesn't seem to be shit-all in the way of authority anywhere.

The van's hood is up and one of the mechanics is underneath with his legs sticking out. His shoes are worn and covered in red mud, which is pretty much what the whole town is made of. The other guy is in the driver's seat. Neither of them has told us their names, and now it's awkward and we don't ask. When he turns the key, the starter motor grinds, then there's silence. This is worse than before. Soon, the battery will give out. I'm worried the mechanics might not know what they're doing. But seeing as I have no idea what the problem is, I'm not about to tell them what to do.

"Ain't getting no gas," says the mechanic in the driver's seat. "Fittin' install a new electronic pump."

Two hours later, the van's running. We get the band up and out of the motel room, and we're back on the road. It's now late afternoon. If we push it, we can still make tonight's show in Baton Rouge. Chris is driving. We're making good time. The passing countryside is rice paddies, fields of leafy green soybeans, swamp ash, and palm trees. It's muggy and hot as hell. A helicopter roars dangerously close over the highway and I'm thinking this is what Vietnam must be like.

We've been on the road for twenty minutes and heading over a small hill when the engine sputters and dies. We coast down into another small town and roll to a stop in an old gas station parking lot.

Welcome to Eudora.

Two white guys are working on a dented green pickup. They're in bib overalls and red baseball caps. We get out of the van. They stare at us. It feels like the exact opposite of Lake Village.

"Something's wrong with our van," I say to one of the white guys. I notice the other one is standing on a wooden box. He's a midget, or a dwarf. I can never remember the difference.

"What's wrong with it?" asks, the non-dwarf white guy, who later turns out to be Whitey, the garage owner.

"Not getting any gas," Chris tells him.

"Not getting' gas, how?" Whitey asks, his accent thick and hard to decipher.

"Carburetor. The gas ain't getting to the carburetor."

"You drove in here, didn't cha?"

Chris explains how we'd broken down in Lake Village, the mechanics there had installed a new electronic fuel pump, and that we'd made it down the road to here, but now it was doing the same thing again. No gas.

"Ain't no mechanic in Lake Village," says Whitey.

No one says it, but there's an underlining current to our conversation. We're strangers, liars, untrustworthy, and Whitey is suspicious of our motives.

"Think you can fix it?"

"I can take a look," says Whitey as he walks back to the pickup truck he was working on.

We all stand there and watch as he leans under the truck's hood wrenching some unseen bolt, ignoring us.

The sun is setting. Long shadows cross the road and birds are everywhere, flying between trees and making a ruckus. The guys are stressing about the show in Baton Rouge. Roche is on the pay phone calling the club. Chris and I unhitch the trailer and chain it to a fence pole. Then we get the van started and pull it up to the garage door, in the hopes that Whitey will soon "take a look."

"There a motel around here?" I ask the dwarf (we later find out his named is Peanut). But he just scoffs and spits on the ground as way of answering my question.

Roche is talking with Whitey, asking if he knows anybody that'd like to make some money driving the band to Baton Rouge. Whitey says he'll call a buddy of his, Buford. See if he'll ask Eudora's patriarch, a Mr. Baker—and apparently the only guy in town who drives something other than a pickup truck—if he'd drive the band to Baton Rouge in his van.

"It'll cost ya though," says Whitey. "Any time you deal with Mr. Baker... it costs."

An hour later, Mr. Baker drives up in a plush twelve-seater van with Buford riding shotgun in the passenger seat.

"Got a plane that'll hold four if in y'all want to fly," says Mr. Baker. "But it's getting dark and I don't see so good no more."

"No fuckin' way," says Joe Wood. "I ain't getting in no plane with a blind guy."

Mr. Baker owns the local crop-dusting service and a few other things in Eudora. Whitey and Buford bow down to him. The dwarf doesn't even rate his acknowledgement. Apparently, Mr. Baker is the only man here with a last name as everyone else is referred to by their first name.

After negotiating a fee, basically the band's guarantee from the night's show, they all cram into the van, and Chris and I watch them drive away. The plan is we stay here and as soon as Whitey fixes the problem, we drive on down to Baton Rouge and pick them up, hopefully in time to get us all to the next show.

Whitey and Peanut roll the pickup truck inside and pull down the sliding garage door. Then they disappear around the side of the building. Ten minutes later Whitey pulls up in a blue pickup.

"See ya in the morning," he says, and drives off.

We walk around the side of the building just in time to see Peanut lock the gate to a fenced-in yard behind the garage. Our trailer has been moved inside the yard, and I wonder how they moved it when we'd locked it to the fence. Then I see our chain and padlock lying in the grass. It's been cut with a bolt cutter.

The midget puts on a motorcycle helmet and hops on a small Vespa-like scooter, which he kickstarts, revs the gas, and nods to us before he drives off in the opposite direction as Whitey.

When it all quiets down, the crickets kick in, the noise suddenly deafening.

Chris and I are stuck here. The van isn't working. The band has left us some money. It's night. There's no motel. We haven't eaten all day.

We walk down the road to the mini-mart we passed on the way into town and buy a case of beer.

Hung over, tired, stiff from sleeping on the floor of the van, I wake to Whitey and Peanut arguing. My mouth is dry and tastes like crap. I light a cigarette and get out, hoping Whitey will open the garage so I can use the bathroom to take a shit. Chris and I stayed up most of the night, sitting on the bench in the front of the garage, drinking beers, playing guitars, and smoking cigarettes. About midnight a cop pulled up. Asked what we thought we were doing here. Told him we'd broken down, that Whitey was going to fix our van tomorrow.

I'm hoping that's true.

It's only 8AM, the temperature is already in the high nineties, and the humidity has already got me soaking wet. Whitey, who of course showered and changed clothes, is looking fresh, wearing brand new blue and white striped bib overalls, a Razorbacks T-shirt, and an odd red cloth hat I've only seen worn in the South.

"Fittin' to see what y'all talkin' 'bout," says Whitey.

At first, I'm not sure what Whitey is saying and then realize he means fixing the van. For the next hour, Chris and I stand around in the hot sun while Whitey pokes at the motor and Peanut hovers around handing him tools. Both of them endlessly jabber on about yesterday's baseball game and some girl named Martha who may or may not be "putting out." I'm hoping for that "ah ha" moment where Whitey discovers what the hell is wrong with the van, and we finally have a solution and can get the hell out of here, which just doesn't seem to be happening. Neither of them appears to be in a hurry about anything. Whitey has yet to unlock the office with the bathroom, and I still have to take a shit. The other gas station is a short walk away, and we tell Whitey we'll be back. He grunts in our direction. The dwarf smiles and waves.

We slowly amble on down the one lane of cracked and crumbling asphalt to the Double Quick mini-mart that's on the actual highway, State Route 65. We say howdy to the same guy who was behind the counter yesterday and ask to use his restroom. He yes and it's surprisingly clean. I take the time to wash my face and run a quick finger over my teeth. I really need to brush them but I'm hoping we'll be out of here soon and we can stop at a real truck stop with a shower and edible food. Maybe even find a strong cup of coffee.

What passes as "food" at the Double Quick leaves a lot to be desired. They got a pile of fried chicken that I'm pretty sure had been there last night. A big glass jar of pickled eggs, another of pigs feet, and there's an entire rack devoted to different brands of spicy pork rinds. Southern food, at its best, is an acquired taste. Small town mini-mart Southern food is a whole other dimension and unless you've a hankering for all things breaded and fried, you're shit out of luck. In desperation, we grab a couple of chicken biscuit sandwiches and the breakfast drink of choice throughout the Midwest and the South, Mountain Dew.

Mid-afternoon, Whitey throws up his hands and calls it a day. "The missus got Saturday dinner, family coming over," and just like that he's driving off in his pickup. Peanut stands around making small talk and eyeing our pile of beer cans from last night. "You gonna redeem them?" We tell him no and he gleefully smashes each one flat and kicks them all into a garbage bag.

"Best be buyin' your beer for tomorrow. No sale, come Sunday."

"What you talking about, Peanut?"

"Double Quick don't sell beer on Sunday. Nobody do in Chicot County. You gotta go clean way over Greenville. That Mississippi. They even gots a pool hall."

"How you think we get anywhere without a van?"

"Just sayin'."

"Thanks, Peanut. Appreciate you letting us know. Hoping Whitey fixes the damn van tomorrow and we can get the hell out of here. Right?"

"Sunday's church. You a blasphemer?"

"What?"

Peanut doesn't respond. He's too busy attaching his bag of empties with bungee cords to the back of his moped.

"Whitey's coming in tomorrow, right Peanut?"

Peanut puts his helmet on and, without his usual nod of the head, slowly putts off.

"What the fuck!"

We buy two cases of beer at the Double Quick. The guy behind the counter wants to know if we're throwing a party. He laughs at his own joke and then spits tobacco juice into a cup next to the register. We also buy a loaf of bread, American cheese, bologna, and small jar of yellow mustard. I can't even look at anything fried, greasy, or breaded right now. I'd mug a small child for a salad and I don't even eat salads. I want something fresh that doesn't come in a paper sack with grease stains or a Styrofoam container overflowing with white gravy. Chris throws on three packs of smokes and bag of ice. Without talking about it, we're both obviously resigned to the fact we may be here for a lot longer than planned.

An hour and six beers later, two cars full of teenagers pull up to Whitey's garage. "Y'all the punk rockers?" one of them yells. He looks like a jock, only he's wearing a Black Sabbath T-shirt. There're three girls with him, two in short shorts and cut-off T-shirts showing taut stomachs and a lot of skin. The other's more like a tomboy with gray sweats and big white Nikes. The second car is all dudes, backwards baseballs caps and baggy shorts and oversized T-shirts. "Where y'all from?"

"Los Angeles," says Chris, as he lights a cigarette.

"L.A., huh?"

"What y'all doin' here?" The girl's got a dirty blonde head of hair and is somewhat attractive. She runs a hand across her exposed stomach and smiles in our direction.

"Van broke down," I say. "Whitey's fixing it."

"Y'all drinkin' beer?" The jock's got a half pint of bourbon in his hand and big grin on his face. He waves the pint in the air. "I ain't got no time for beer." All the kids laugh. He's obviously the alpha male, and an absolute younger version of Whitey.

"You related to Whitey?" I ask.

The kid ignores my question. "We fittin' to head over Greenville way, y'all wanna tag along?"

The cop abruptly turns the corner and cruises by real slow. The jock kid hides the pint behind his back, smiles, and waves. The cop waves and stares real hard at Chris and me. I'm thinking nothing about this is going to turn out good. I glance over at Chris. He meets my gaze. "Nah, thanks. We're going to stay here."

The jock kid chugs his pint and tosses the empty against the side of the garage. It breaks in shards that fall across the cement steps. "Suit yo self, but you might be stayin' longer than you thought."

I haven't shot any dope since Oklahoma City. Oddly enough I'm not really hurting. Sometimes it's just like that. Your kick is negligible either due to circumstances and environment, you weren't using that heavy, or maybe the planets are just aliened in your favor. Other than the occasional diarrhea and sleeping badly, both of which I can blame on being stuck here in Eudora, I'm doing okay.

But I am restless knowing I'm going to spend another night drinking beers until I pass out. It sucks. I almost regret not getting in the car with Whitey's kid and heading on over to Greenville. At least it would have been a change of scenery.

"Come on, man. Let's see the rest of Eudora."

Small towns at 10PM, Saturday night or no Saturday night, are dead. We walk down single lane streets with the occasional house on both sides, their lights off and dogs barking. At an intersection with train tracks, we make a left and head deeper into a wooded area with even fewer houses, no streetlights, and the road turns to dirt.

"Must be the suburbs," I joke.

When we pass a boarded-up storefront with a weed-filled parking lot, the houses get shabbier. Their porches are sagging and in the front yards there are discarded refrigerators, old washing machines, and dusty, old cars with flat tires. Every house has a large, nasty dog that barks ferociously, straining at its leash and lunging for us as we pass.

We're about to turn back when we hear music and people shouting, like they're partying and having fun. Way down the street there's a one-story building with a bright yellow light above the entrance and cars parked outside. I'm momentarily blinded from staring at the light when a man materializes out of the dark and stumbles toward us.

"What in hell y'all doin'?" He's wearing a bright red suit, striped blue tie, wide-brimmed furry hat, and those black and white saddle shoes you see in old movies. We're standing in ninety-plus degree heat with at least one hundred percent humidity. I'm drenched in sweat and I'm in jeans and a cut-off T-shirt.

"Y'all on wrong side-a-the-tracks," he says. "Where in hell you from?"

"California."

"Los Angeles."

"L.A.! Y'all brought the stank with you, right?"

"Excuse me?"

"Y'all smoke, or what?"

"I smoke Camels, why?"

"Nah, talkin' bout righteous bush, fool."

A beat up Oldsmobile slowly cruises past. The couple inside waves to the man in the suit and the woman calls out, "Bo, why y'all messin' with them white boys?"

"Ain't messin' with nobodies. Mine your business." Bo holds up the smallest joint I've ever seen. "Y'all wanna smoke some Bo-weed?"

We're huddled together behind the building with the music and bright light, which turns out to be The Continental Club. Bo said it'd be safer to smoke in the back and we followed him through the parked cars along a dirt alley to a yard filled with trash and broken furniture. I take a hit on the joint and it tastes like burning straw.

After I exhale, I don't feel a thing, but that's okay because I fucking hate smoking pot—lamest high ever—I'm just trying to be sociable. Bo is insistent we come party with him. "Seein' y'all's from California and all."

"Y'all like music?" Without even waiting for a response, Bo abruptly turns and starts walking away. "Come on," he yells over his shoulder.

We follow Bo through an unmarked door into a large barroom that's so dark it takes a second for my eyes to adjust. Red lights run along the side of the room, a small stage off to the left, and several round tables have been pushed out of the way to clear the dance floor. The place is absolutely packed and as soon as we enter everything stops. The loud music gets cut off, people are staring, and the room goes completely silent. I'm getting some hostile glares from the dudes at the bar and realize Chris and I are the only white people in the room. When a beautiful woman in a tight dress with mountains of cleavage smiles at me, I smile back and start to relax.

"Hey y'all. Stop the drama. They's from L.A." Bo puts his arms around me and shoves us through the crowd toward the bar. Everyone laughs and the music starts up again. It's old soul. Marvin Gaye's "Got to Give It Up." When Marvin sings, "I used to go out to parties," everyone shouts and raises their arms in air. They're all dancing and laughing. Bodies are rubbing, and it's a good time. A man with dreads hands me a cold beer, says, "Howdy, welcome to Eudora," and the beautiful woman with the amazing cleavage smiles even more. I light a cigarette and follow Bo farther down the bar. Chris is behind me, talking to a couple of guys and they've given him a beer. I'm hanging with Bo as he introduces me around. I keep sneaking glances at the beautiful woman and she keeps smiling my way.

A man dressed in baggy pants and a Prince T-shirt slaps money on the bar and yells, "Everyone's drinkin'!" I get handed a plastic cup of clear liquid that burns my throat when I take a sip.

Folks are toasting me and asking about California, wondering do we all really have swimming pools in our backyards and what's with the damn earthquakes? A young girl with Jheri curls asks how I get my hair all spikey and, "stand up like it do." I look back around for the beautiful women, but she's gone. After all that eye flirting, I feel like a fool for not at least saying hello. Another man shoves a drink in my hand. I'm starting to catch a real buzz.

Sometime around 4AM, Travis, a friend of Bo's, drops us off at Whitey's and then speeds away in his Chevy Nova. "Ain't fittin' to be caught out here at night."

I'm shit-faced drunk and so is Chris. We're laughing and smoking cigarettes, sitting on Whitey's front steps. The cop drives by, slows down and waves, and that makes us laugh even more.

"We're locals now."

I wake up with a pounding headache. Birds are chirping, it's sunny as hell, and I momentarily don't know where I am. Then it all comes back like a freight train into my aching brain. I'm lying in the van and we're still in Eudora.

I get out and stretch. The gas station is locked and no one's here. Not even Peanut. I walk around back and take a piss in the tall grass behind the building. I'm not sure what time it is, but I'm pretty sure it's late in the morning and Whitey not being here sucks. Does Whitey really take the Sabbath off?

Back at the van, Chris is just getting up. "I think we're fucked," I say.

"How so? Well, besides the obvious fucked-ness of all this." Chris gestures with his hand as if displaying the wonders of Eudora and Whitey's garage.

"I do believe, like Peanut said, Whitey is *fittin'* to go to church on Sunday. Then there's probably Sunday dinner. God knows there may even be Sunday Bible study dinner. The fuckin' dude ain't coming in today, man."

"If Whitey is such a good Christian, how come there's no 'Bring the stranded punks home to dinner'? 'Oh lord, they must be starving'... but no."

"I'd settle for a shower and a decent toilet."

The beer is warm, all the ice melted, and cooler is full of tepid water. Neither of us feels like walking all the way down to the Double Quick for more ice. We just sit on Whitey's front steps and drink it warm all day until the sun begins to set and the cicadas start their screeching in the trees.

"I can't be having y'all sittin' front of my garage all day and night," says Whitey.

"Well, good morning to you too, Whitey." What I really want to say is fix the damn van and we won't be sitting here, and why the hell didn't you fix it yesterday?

"Peanut, let's do this."

Whitey's got on a new pair of dark blue bib overalls and John Deere baseball cap. He's rolled the gleaming brand new tool chest out of the garage and is digging into the motor with a new-found earnestness.

"Peanut? Need you to hop on yo moped and gets me some auto parts."

"You sure 'bout that?"

"I'm 'bout to engage in some midget abuse if'in you don't."

Chris and I walk down to the Double Quick for cigarettes. We don't buy a case of beer and the guy behind the counter says, "What, party over?" I'm so fucking tired of Eudora—the guy behind the counter, Peanut and Whitey, the damn cop who drives by all night, and drinking warm beer.

Whitey's got the van running when we get back and it sounds great. Chris pays Whitey way too much money, but that's the price he asks. Without saying goodbye, we hook the trailer up and drive as fast as we can out of town. Neither of us even bothered to ask what was wrong with the van or what Whitey did to fix it. "Fuck you, Eudora!" I yell out the window and light a smoke.

***

Toms River, New Jersey. We're playing an all-ages early show at a VFW hall and there's a ton of punks lined up outside. I count at least thirty Misfit T-shirts (it is New Jersey after all), a smattering of Catholic girls in super short plaid skirts with torn fishnets, several serious mohawks, and the prerequisite of assorted metalheads wearing Motörhead T-shirts, and that one confused guy in a Depeche Mode t-shirt.

Load-in is easy. The VFW hall is a one-story building with a side door straight off the parking lot. We're all in the dressing room waiting for the promoter to bring the pizza and beer. It's fucking hot as hell and just as humid. Ron's playing his guitar and Roche and Joe are arguing.

Mitch Dean, the self-appointed de facto band manager, is pacing the floor, stressing out and being incredibly annoying. No one has actually said that Mitch Dean is the manager, but for some reason he's decided that he's in control, even though I road manage most of the bands I work with. The guys in T.S.O.L. are so paranoid of getting ripped off that they do all the logistics and finances themselves, which is a bad call. A road manager takes care of all the small shit and has to make decisions, and not all of them are pleasant. When the road manager is a band member, it usually comes off as if they're trying to call the shots, which is exactly what Mitch Dean is trying to do. Plus, Mitch Dean thinks he's better than everyone else. He isn't strung-out on heroin, mainly because he's afraid of heroin. Instead he drinks rum and Cokes every night and chases underage girls.

Mitch's biggest bone of contention is Chris and I drove to New Orleans after Eudora instead of heading straight to Florida to catch up with the band. They had to spend the money to fly to Atlanta where we eventually hooked back up with them at the Metroplex. Worst part of that being the band was picked up at the airport in a limo and when they pulled up in front of the club a lot of punks were pissed off. Nothing says "sell out" like a punk band stepping out of a limo—not that Mitch Dean was worried about that—but Roche and Ron sure as hell were.

"I'm not paying you guys," said Mitch.

"We sat in Eudora for four days," I said. "You fuckin' owe us."

Tonight is another all-ages gig. Ticket prices are low and we're not going to make shit, and Mitch is stressing. The fact that he has to pay us our weekly salary is pissing him off and he's looking for any excuse not to. Not to mention Mitch is from New Jersey and, oddly enough, he's added no names to the guest list.

After the show the band disappears to the comfort of the air-conditioned motel. Chris and I grab a half pint of whiskey and walk down to the boardwalk.

It's a Saturday night and crowded, there's really loud music, and we can barely push through the throngs of people standing around. When we get to the actual boardwalk, there's a stage set up with amps and a drum kit and a lot of guys with big hair. It's a total heavy metal scene and when the band hits the stage, camera crews appear and rush forward.

We're in the middle of a fucking video shoot. The band is Bon Jovi. They're all lip-syncing. None of the amps are actually on. The same song is repeatedly pumped through the PA as the band pretends to play their instruments. The crowd is going wild. They don't care it's fake; they've got their arms in the air and are jumping around and excited. Bon Jovi, hometown New Jersey boys making the big time.

Then it's another take, another pose, another pouty lip-sync, another panoramic shot of wind machine-blown big hair and stage theatrics. The makeup girls are on standby. There's a craft table with snacks. An ambulance is parked alongside the stage just in case one of the guys break a fingernail. Off to the side are a bunch of cops. One of them sees the half pint in my back pocket and tells me I can't drink here in public.

"I wasn't drinking it," I tell him.

He doesn't like my attitude. "Don't give me lip, fella."

The crowd pushes us all back against one another. Chris and I are now right next to him. The cop turns his back on us and makes a joke to his fellow cops. "Fuckin' hair looks like they put a finger in a light socket."

Chris reaches over and grabs the butt of the cop's revolver in his holster and pulls on it. The cop spins around. He looks surprised and a little scared. I pull Chris back from the cop and into the crowd.

"You're not untouchable, motherfucker," screams Chris.

The crowd closes in around us and surges toward the stage as the band comes back for another round. The cops try to push their way through but it's too packed. I keep pulling Chris by the arm until we're on the other side of the boardwalk.

"What the fuck, Chris?"

"I fuckin' hate cops."

***

Stuck in traffic in the Holland Tunnel in the middle of a summer day is its own kind of special hell. We're six smelly guys packed in a van and the traffic's not moving. Even though we're from California and should be prepared for hot weather, the air conditioner doesn't work. I don't know what's worse, having the windows up and suffocating, or open with a slight breeze and breathing all the exhaust fumes.

We finally exit out into the city and head down Spring Street. But the traffic is not much better than the tunnel. The band is headed to a hotel in Queens the promoter booked for them. The show isn't until tomorrow night, and I'm not about to cross the river and leave N.Y.C. to just sit around a hotel room. Chris and I grab our bags, step out of the van at a stoplight, and tell the guys we'll catch up to them tomorrow. The situation with Mitch Dean has gotten on both our nerves. We need time away from the band.

A quick taxi ride and we're on 3rd Street heading to Denise Ondayko's dingy basement apartment across from the Hells Angels. A couple of the lookouts eye us suspiciously as we walk down the block carrying duffle bags. We say hey to Denise, stash our bags, and immediately head out to score.

I'm nodding out in a small brick alcove of Denise's apartment, most likely a former broom closet that passes for a bedroom. There's a small twin mattress fitting snuggly inside, leaving no room for much else. It's early morning, like 6AM early, and I can't figure out why the hell I'm awake. But when I'm really loaded, I don't exactly sleep. I just sort of nod out all night, constantly waking up, smoking, and nodding back out—hopefully without a lit cigarette in my hand.

Only this morning it's different and I have the urge to get up and go outside. The room feels confining. I slip on my clothes and grab cigarettes and money. Maybe I'll get a cup of that notoriously bad N.Y.C. deli coffee served in those weird blue paper cups with Greek writing on the side. Not even sure when I last ate. An egg sandwich might be in order, too.

It's unmercifully hot in the lobby. I open the front door and a cool breeze hits me in the face. I step outside and light a cigarette. The entire street is filled with cops with guns. They're all wearing dark windbreakers with FBI, ATF or DEA embossed in huge white letters on the back. N.Y.C.'s finest is also there in uniform. A SWAT team dressed in black tactical gear runs past with M16s at the ready and charges the Hells Angels' front door. The door is busted open with a resounding thud and hordes of various cops start piling inside, all of them yelling. A woman screams and more cops push forward to gain entrance.

I catch the eye of an FBI agent standing ten feet away. He's got a gun in his hand and looks at me questioningly. I'm wearing the usual cut-off black T-shirt, black Levi's, and motorcycle boots, which is probably not a whole hell of a lot different than what the majority of the Hells Angels they're busting are wearing.

I casually drop my cigarette and crush it with the toe of my boot. Being careful to not make any sudden moves, I slowly head back inside—worried the Fed will try and stop me. By the time the lobby door shuts, I'm already out the back door. I really don't have time for this shit today. I've got to buy a white dress shirt. My sister, Scott, is getting married.

City Island is way the hell out in the Bronx. It takes two subways and a bus to get there, and I'm only somewhat sure I know where I'm going. I did buy a pressed white dress shirt that still had dry cleaning tags at a used clothing store. I even wiped the crud off my boots and put on the cleanest pair of pants I own.

I shoot one bag of dope before leaving and I have another in my pocket just in case I get sick. I nod through the two subway rides and wake up when I hit Pelham Bay.

My entire family is there when I arrive. The wedding is in the backyard. It's beautiful day, warm but not too hot, a little overcast, which is actually good, as no one wants to stand outside in the sun. My sister looks beautiful. Neil looks stressed, but then he always does. Everyone is well dressed and, for the most part, appears well off and I feel totally out of place. I am a junkie on the road, touring with another band that no one here knows or even cares about. My life is so removed from the reality of these successful professionals.

I'm uncomfortable and looking around for a drink and, for the next few hours, I don't stray too far from the bar.

T.S.O.L. is playing the Rock Hotel. The show has already started and I'm late. Front door security gives me a shitload of grief. It's New York City. They've heard every bullshit excuse from people trying to get into a show. I tell them I'm T.S.O.L.'s roadie. I was at my sister's wedding. Why the fuck else would I be wearing a white dress shirt? I'm about to punch this really big dude who could easily kill me when the promoter Chris Williamson comes outside. I know Williamson from Kennedys show at The World.

"Hey Chris, I'm with T.S.O.L. Tell your man to let me in."

Williamson barely acknowledges me, says, "Let him in," and hands me a backstage pass. I'm pushing through the crowd to the stage. It's packed full of skinheads, Sid Vicious look-a-likes, and a lot of big hair. D.O.A. is headlining, Gang Green is second on the bill, and The Dicks have already opened the show. T.S.O.L. has the middle slot after The Dicks and they're not too happy about not headlining.

I'm backstage trying to find the dressing room when I run into Debbie Gordon, The Dicks' manager. "You look like shit. You're fucking wasted."

"Thanks, Debbie." My words are garbled and I can barely keep my eyes open.

I find the backstage and immediately head to the bathroom. I quickly shoot the remaining bag of dope, hoping that'll get me a little more adjusted. I end up nodding out on the toilet with the needle still in my arm.

I wake up to loud banging on the door. I push my way through a line of angry punks who need to take a piss. "Get the fuck out of my way."

The band is already on stage tuning up. I'm seeing double and can barely focus. I'm having trouble keeping my balance. I bounce off the hallway walls and then I'm on stage. I trip on a cord and fall into Ron as he's tuning his guitar. He calls me a jerk and to watch where I'm going.

I stumble off behind the PA side-fills and nod out. When I come to, the band is playing. It's loud. The stage is filled with punks skanking away and knocking over gear. A stagediver gets caught up in Ron's guitar cord and jumps off into the audience, ripping it out of his guitar. I somehow retrieve the cord and untangle it. I'm standing in the middle of the stage, a good three feet away from Ron, the cord in my hand. But I can't coordinate the movement to actually plug it in.

Mitch Dean throws a drumstick that flies by my head. He's screaming something I can't hear. I'm the walking dead poster child of excessive drug abuse. I shouldn't even be up on stage. I'm too fucking loaded.

This will be my last tour with T.S.O.L.

2009. T.S.O.L. is playing Slim's, a club in San Francisco's SOMA district. Maïe Maïshka is visiting from Lyon, and she and Anna Lisa drag me down to the show. It's not like I don't want to go. It's just that I don't really go to shows anymore. I have no idea what to do at a venue when I'm not working. And more to the point I've just completed grad school. I'm about to move to L.A. and I'm trying to pack and get the hell out of town. But, hey, it's T.S.O.L. and I haven't seen them in years.

The club is full to capacity with aging punkers and really young kids who weren't even born when Dance with Me *was first released. Jack is back with Ron and Roche, and they have a new drummer named Tiny. The last time I saw them was outside a show nine years earlier when I was struggling to stay clean in rehab. Sitting in their rented motorhome parked behind Maritime Hall on Harrison Street, they all told me they were in recovery, and it sort of took away the stigma of being a newcomer... Well, sort of. Here were people I love and respect and they had gotten sober. Maybe I could too?*

Yet tonight it feels different. I've got eight years clean and even though I still feel awkward at shows, it's really good to see how well all of us are doing. How healthy and happy we all look. After load-out we stand outside in the street shooting the shit and I realize just how much I miss these guys. All the time I spent in a van with Ron and Roche and how much their friendship means to me. Listening to Jack laugh. Watching the youngsters surround him in awe. For just a millisecond I'm transported back. And right in that moment I miss the road.

THIS COULD BE ANYWHERE (THIS COULD BE EVERYWHERE) 1985: DEAD KENNEDYS

Dead Kennedys are doing North America in a big way. We're going out on the road for three months. Kris Carleson is still the road manager. Ron, Chris, and I are the road crew, and we hired a new girl, Alex Teare, to sell T-shirts with Anna Lisa.

We rent an oversized diesel Iveco. It's an Italian box truck, larger than a package van, but not the full-sized, cumbersome twenty-six-foot truck. With big, plush seats and a crew cab, there's still only room for four up front. It's going to be tight. There is a sliding door from the cab that accesses the cargo area, and we decide to utilize some of that space for a "crew lounge."

Chris and I find a wood-framed couch at a thrift store. We cut the legs off and screw it into the floor of the truck bed, about six feet into the cargo area facing toward the cab, effectively splitting the space into two sections. We hang several large packing blankets from the ceiling and attach them to either side to seal in whatever heat will be coming in from the cab. There are no windows and it's dark. I can't see my hand in front of my face. Chris installs a light—a bare bulb that hangs from the ceiling—that sort of helps. But it still feels like a holding cell. At least now there's room for the crew. The rest of the space is for gear and merchandise.

The Kennedys' gear has always been minimal. Klaus literally brings his bass, an amp, and a homemade speaker cabinet. Ray has two Marshall amps, a Marshall cabinet, and a footlocker case with two guitars, an Echoplex, and cords. D.H.'s Rogers kit: a kick, two floor toms, a snare, two rack toms, a hi-hat, and three cymbals in aging black fiber road cases. They are constantly falling apart, and we are continuously duct taping them back together.

These days it's the T-shirts that require all the needed room. We're selling a shit-ton of shirts. When we play small towns, the punks come out of nowhere and every one of them buys a shirt. There is nothing better than a Dead Kennedys T-shirt to piss off that certain authoritarian figure in their lives. Leslie Jambor has set up her silk-screening shop, Black Wave, at Alternative Tentacles in S.F., and she's printing shirts as fast as we can sell them.

We hit the road for a few warm-up shows in California before heading across country. The band flies everywhere now, and usually separately. Biafra and Ray barely interact, except when they absolutely have to, or when they're performing on stage. The tension between them is bad. Often Klaus and Ray travel together. Carleson deals with Biafra's travel logistics. Once in a while, D.H. will ride with the crew.

Our first show is in San Louis Obispo, and it turns into a riot. Kids were stagediving for the opening bands—nothing but the usual mayhem of a punk show. The S.L.O.P.D. goes apeshit. It turns into a full-fledged police riot. The show gets shut down. We don't even make it back to the venue from the motel and have to wait until the dust settles to retrieve the gear.

The next night we're in Riverside at the De Anza Theater. Cease Fire and Love Canal are the opening bands. I know most of the stage crew from when I lived with Taters in Buena Park. It's cool to hang out with Steve Cunningham and Arab. The stage is complete mayhem, and the audience out for blood. Police in riot gear show up and crack heads. The audience fights back, the venue is getting destroyed, and the promoter starts freaking out. We finish the show before the cops shut it down.

At load-out, out I'm already exhausted and the tour hasn't even started yet.

***

Boise is hosting a law enforcement convention of some sort. The parking lot of every motel we pass is full of cop cars from all over the Northwest. I'm getting anxious and really I just want to sleep before we load-in. I'm hoping our motel will let us check in early. Of course, Carleson could've called ahead and made that happen, but she's asleep in the back, and I'm even more resentful that she's the road manager. The only saving grace is Chris has a bunch of coke. If nothing else, we can get gacked and stay awake until the show.

"I don't wanna leave this room," says Chris.

"I know." I light a cigarette and lick my lips.

There're a dozen small bindles splayed across the bed and he's unfolding and scraping the insides of each with a razorblade, trying to get the last residue of powder into the spoon on the nightstand.

"See all the cops at the Holiday Inn?"

Another flick of the razorblade, another empty bindle tossed. Fine white powder barely covers the inside of the spoon. A final offering. Penance for the last hit.

"We need more."

"That's an understatement."

The room is dark. The curtains are closed. The TV is off. The only light is from the bedside lamp. The rest of the crew is at the venue. We've been shooting coke for hours. I'm nervous. My thoughts are racing. My mouth is dry.

The rush is small: a fleeting taste, a minor numb, the high-pitched feedback faint in my ears.

I fucking hate coke.

But I want more.

I always want more.

"Come on, we gotta go."

"Yeah, yeah, okay."

The streetlights above the motel parking lot are way too bright, invading the night sky, which is endless and full of stars. A distant loud noise makes me flinch. My nerves are on edge. I watch a passing car as I fumble for my pack of cigarettes and then my lighter. I'm going through motions as if on cruise control.

"Ever think about what you're doing?"

"Mean like getting high?"

"No, I mean like what are we doing here."

"As in the philosophical, 'What are we doing here'?"

"Another night, another show, another town full of wasted kids, and we're just a blip in the timeline of nothing, going nowhere."

"Dude, shut the fuck up."

"I'm serious."

"I know. That's why I said shut the fuck up. You're going all cosmic weird on me."

"Just want shit to mean more."

"Then make it have meaning. Do something that'll change it."

"Maybe I will."

A solitary phone booth, its interior light glowing and inviting, sits at the corner. A quarter dropped in the slot dings and chimes on its way down.

"Hello? Police? Yeah... I planted a bomb in the name of god. Yeah, that's right, a bomb, at the show with all them goddamn punk rockers. Kill 'em all. Jesus died for your sins. Not mine!"

The sound of the receiver slamming against the payphone echoes across the street. A block away a truck passes, its muffler coughing and loud. The night becoming quiet as it fades away.

"What the fuck, man?"

The street's empty. Everything is closed, the shops are dark and no one else is out here. Another eight minutes and there are sirens in the distance—a lot of sirens. They're coming towards us.

"You really just call 911?"

"Nah. That was a joke."

"Good, because I think I hear a million fuckin' cops."

"That's just the coke going away."

I light a cigarette and pass the pack to Chris.

Out front of the concert hall there's at least ten squad cars, emergency lights flashing. A dozen cops stand around talking into radios, doing nothing. Punks are crowding the sidewalk—some drifting across the street. Small groups huddle by a parking lot. A fire engine pulls to the curb. Firefighters in large overcoats, rubber boots, and helmets rush into the building. The prevailing atmosphere strangely quiet and morose.

In the alley, at the rear stage door, a large, scruffy security guard stops us. "Can't let you in. Bomb threat."

"No shit?"

"This shit happens a lot in Boise?"

***

Omaha-fucking-Nebraska—geographically about as mid-America as you can get—1,745 miles from San Francisco, 1,250 miles from New York—and there's no heroin. We had hoped the drugs we brought would get us through the rural areas until we hit a major metropolis with a thriving heroin trade. Only a week into the tour and we're already out.

It's day two and, as kicking goes, things are pretty good. Made it through the show at the Omaha Civic Auditorium Music Hall. Being a union venue, I didn't have to do shit. We unload the gear at the back door. Union dudes lug it inside. We set it up on stage. During the show, big dudes manned the barricades and there were cops everywhere, which sucked as it was repressive as hell. But there were no stagedivers or fights and I got to relax. The venue had a real place to sell T-shirts and, best of all, no goddamn guest list to deal with. *Who the fuck knows anybody in Omaha?*

I practically sleepwalk through the show, then breakdown the gear. The union guys load us out. We say, "Thanks!" They say, "Come back anytime." We all shake hands and then load our stuff into the truck. Wish every night was this easy.

I've been drinking beers all night, hoping to dull the withdrawal. The Kennedys have five cases on their rider that never get drunk. There are at least eight cases in the back of the truck we've kept rather than leave behind. We could probably get busted for transporting alcohol across state lines without a permit.

I've been swallowing Valiums all night like they're antacids. I've a dwindling supply, along with some sleeping pills and Darvons. Anna Lisa has her own pills, which we both keep secret and then bitch at each other when they're gone and neither of us shared.

It's only midnight. The streets of Omaha are wide and badly lit. They stretch for miles in straight lines arching over the earth's curve into the distance. The city itself is gray. There are no signs of life and hardly any traffic. A train whistle, far away in the distance, interrupts the quiet. The night sky, full of stars, goes on forever above our heads. Just off the interstate, the motel is a massive four-story prefab steel and aluminum monolith stretching an entire block, every room a highway view. The parking lot could hold a fleet of tour buses.

With nowhere to go and nothing to do, the crew's room becomes the place to be. It's a suite with an adjoining lounge, two large couches, a bar, and a big TV. Ray, Klaus, D.H., Anna Lisa, Chris, Alex, Ron, Carleson, and I are all hanging out and drinking. Biafra isn't with us—he probably ran into an adoring punker who wants an interview for her zine—but none of us seem to notice.

I slip into the bathroom and check my pills. The Darvons and Valiums are gone. I must have taken them, but I still feel like shit. I swallow a handful of Placidyls—big red gel caps that knock you out. All I want to do is not feel like shit. Maybe go to sleep. End this night. I'm starving and want to puke at the same time. Room service is listed as the Steak and Ale restaurant, a quasi-fast food joint next door, which closed at 7PM. I feel like some lonely traveling salesman. Out of luck. Out of time.

Our suite's lounge is old, but the furnishings appear brand new. The gaudy wallpaper is bright green with orange stripes. The light fixtures are chrome and smoked gray glass. I'm sprawled on a '60s sectional sofa, one of those blue Naugahyde and dark stained wood frame numbers. It'll be called retro-modern in twenty years. I have a warm beer that's gone flat. I'm watching everyone; they're laughing and talking—these are people I like and consider my friends. I might even care too much about some of them. A few I even love. But I'm kicking heroin in Omaha and all I can think about is scoring dope and getting well.

My muscles tense, my stomach turns, my mind flips and falters. My thoughts race to strange conclusions. It's like I'm a TV with its horizontal on the fritz—an old-fashioned black and white Mutual of Omaha, my *Wild Kingdom*, a Marlin Perkins reject, the survival of the fittest. Right down the road from Father Flanagan's Boys Town. I'm feeling more like a Dead End Boy than the Dead Boys. I'm wishing Spencer Tracy would come give me some drugs. No, not drugs, heroin. I'm standing on the precipice, looking down into the Continental Divide. Council Bluffs. Just east of here. If the Great Plains break off, it'll all slide west downhill into the ocean. Where there's heroin, the West Coast is full of heroin. But then so is the East Coast, but that's up hill. Like marching ants. Ant hills. The middle of America. Call me a cab. I want to take a train home. No, a plane. Yeah, a plane. I want to fly home for heroin.

Klaus is staring at me. He looks concerned. I want to tell him it's okay and I've got it figured out. I want to say, "Klaus, I'm flying home, home for heroin," but the words are stuck in my throat. There's a tremor, sort of an earthquake. My legs are shaking. I'm shaking. I'm not cold. But I'm shivering. My throat is dry, so dry, and I want to drink my beer, only it's no longer in my hand, and the shaking continues. Chris is standing over me, so is Anna Lisa. Hey, Anna Lisa, it's going to be all right, I'm flying home. Just stop the fucking earthquake, make it stop.

Shaking. Fucking shaking.

They're lifting me off the sofa. I want to help. I want to say something. I want to ask why. Ray is talking, his lips move, it's mumbled, or I'm mumbled. I want to tell him it's okay, don't bother, whatever it is, don't worry man, don't bother, it's no bother, really.

The hallway is long, it stretches for miles, looks gray like the streets outside, except there's lights, dim lights we pass on the way to the elevator. I'm wondering why they're lifting me up. We going to get food? No worries man, I'm really not that hungry. My feet, useless, drag along the carpet behind me.

We're in the truck. I'm lying between the front seats, my head toward the dash. Streetlights pass above us. It's getting darker. Must be late. Might be too late. It's so fucking cold.

The hospital smells like a hospital. I'm thinking antiseptic. I know its Lysol. I'm thinking the doctors are going to give me drugs. I'm hoping for morphine, but more likely Dilaudids. Please don't give me codeine. I fucking hate it when they give you codeine. Most hospitals are bright. This one's dark and getting darker. The gurney slides along the floor—I'm tired, tired, tired, tired. I want to say goodbye. But nobody's leaving. A nurse stares and doesn't smile. Someone is holding my hand and I think there's never been a more sincere gesture. And then people are moving around me—everywhere, fast, and I feel the wind blow.

8AM—wake up. We have a show in Chicago tomorrow night. I light a cigarette. There's a chemical taste in my mouth. My muscles are unbelievably stiff. I have a headache that won't quit. I get out of bed with an odd memory of running around a drop-in clinic all night. But then I dream a lot of weird shit, so who cares?

"You okay?" asks Anna Lisa.

"Yeah, why wouldn't I be?"

I pack my bag and throw it on the hotel cart with the rest of the bags. Carleson puts her hand on my arm. "You feeling alright?"

"Yeah, let's get out of here."

I still feel like shit. But it's day three of withdrawals, so I'm close to being okay. We'll be in Chicago tonight and there are definitely drugs there. *I can do this.*

Alex and Anna Lisa are tossing the cushions from the couch out the window to Ron down in the parking lot. We need them for the back of the truck to make more sleeping space.

"How ya feeling?" asks Chris.

"Like a million bucks," I say, and wonder why everyone is asking me how I'm doing.

On the way out the door, Carleson unplugs the phone and slips it into her bag. Thankfully there's no mini-bar or that'd be in the truck too. I turn off the lights and we head to the lobby to checkout.

> Symptoms of Placidyl overdose: confusion, reduced coordination, numbness, weakness, loss of muscle control, slurred speech, reduced heartbeat, respiratory depression, and in extreme cases; coma and death. Abbott Laboratories discontinued production in 1999. Although Placidyls could be manufactured by another company

(subject   to   FDA   approval),   no
pharmaceutical company has chosen to
do so.

The Spa is Chicago's Tropicana. It's a rock and roll motel
and we always stay there. A huge, funky three-story motor court on
the north side of town whose "spa" is an algae-infested basement
pool that, like the motel, has seen better days. Although what better
days Chicago has ever had I didn't know. It isn't like there's been a
Las Vegas "Rat Pack" era, and yeah, Al Capone ran the city in
the '20s, but it's 1985, the middle of fucking winter, and Ronald
Reagan's president. Shit be fucked up.

I don't get Chicago. It's like a glorified truck stop in the
middle of the country. It used to be one massive stockyard and the
bad karma ghosts of a trillion slaughtered cows still haunt the place.
There's a near constant wind coming off Lake Michigan. The
projects are prison-like, huge brick high-rises and are everywhere.
The "gold coast" downtown is where all the white folks are—unless
they're hiding in the suburbs—and the local cuisine is greasy hot
beef sandwiches and a double-stuffed deep dish pizza that makes no
goddamn sense. The only saving grace is there's a ton of drugs.
Especially heroin.

We played The Palace Theatre last night. It was sold out.
Criminally Insane, Crucifucks and Naked Raygun opened. Now
we've a day off which means we get to sleep.

I wake up around 8PM. I'm fucking starving and need a shot
of dope. A friend of the promoter's girlfriend helped us score a
quarter ounce of powdery Mexican brown. It's so goddamn good
I'm hoping it lasts until New York. But I'm sure it won't.

I do a quick shot and think about a shower. Anna Lisa is still
asleep and I don't wake her. There's warm unopened beer on the
nightstand. I chug it while getting dressed. The overhead light is way
too bright as I step out into the hall.

Ken Lester showed up unannounced at the show last night and said he was coming on tour with us. Now I have Carleson and Lester to deal with along with the band and crew. Before the show I got chewed out. Ray and Klaus were the last to check out of the motel in Omaha. They got hit with all the charges for the shit we stole from the room. Ray was pissed off. I don't blame him.

"You need shit like that, just buy it. We'll pay for it."

"Sorry, Ray."

I wander the endlessly long halls and run into Alex and D.H. They invite me to come party in D.H.'s room. I tell them no, but thanks. I need something to eat. There's a restaurant and bar on the first floor. I'm trying to find the elevator or even the stairs. On the floor is a medium-sized baggie of white powder. I pick it up. It looks grainy. I think it's someone's laundry detergent. I toss it back on the carpet.

The bar is packed. There's a bunch of good ol' boys drinking and making a lot of noise. They look like the dudes from Black Oak Arkansas or Lynyrd Skynyrd—long hair, beards, and leather vests. It's like some time warp in the '70s, and I'm from the future.

I order a cheeseburger and fries to go, and a beer while I wait. The bartender says, "You with the band? Want me to put it on your tab?"

I'm a little confused. How'd he know I'm with the band? The Kennedys don't run tabs in motel bars for the crew, so I'm pretty sure he's mistaken. "What band?"

The bartender gestures at the country dudes and they all look over at me in unison. "He ain't with us." They all laugh and order another round of rum and Cokes.

The bartender sets an Old Style draft down in front of me and I lean in. "Who the fuck are those yahoos?"

"You didn't see the tour bus in the parking lot?"

"Came in late. Didn't see much."

"That's Greg Allman's band. Or at least his crew."

"Greg Allman's got a tour bus?"

"They played Cubby's last night."

Dead Kennedys played the Palace Theater, which holds about 2,500, and I know the promoter oversold, so probably more like three thousand were in attendance. The club Greg Allman played, The Cubby Bear, holds at maximum one thousand. If Greg Allman is playing venues that small how the hell is he affording a tour bus, and why the fuck don't we have one? Then again if we did, the crew and band would have to travel together. That's just not going to happen.

"You a local?" One of the country boys yells across the bar.

"You talkin' to me?" I point at myself and then shake my head. "No. Why?"

"Where all the women at?"

I shrug my shoulders and go back to drinking my beer. *Why is this burger taking so long?*

"You see that bitch with the bright red hair in here earlier?"

I'm fairly certain they're taking about Alex.

"Bet you'd hit that?"

"Hell yeah I would. Punk bitches be into that kinky sex."

"How you know she punk?"

"Got a damn English accent. Said she's with the Dead Kennedys, or some shit like that."

"The dead what?"

"Punk band."

"Fuckin' fags."

"They on tour?"

"Who's holdin'? Gotta go powder my nose."

"You holding, dumbass."

"Shit."

A huge argument erupts. The good ol' boys start yelling at each other. One of them shoves the one doing all the talking. "I told you in Galveston. Do. Not. Lose. The. Shit. Again. Man!"

The bartender tells them to keep it down or get out. I'm pretty sure they're arguing about drugs. My burger arrives and I remember the baggie lying on the hallway carpet upstairs. I hurry out and take the stairs two at a time. The baggie is gone. I feel stupid I didn't realize what it was.

"Lame-ass Greg Allman's band is staying here."

"Really?" Anna Lisa is sitting naked in our bed. She stretches her arms and exposes the moon and star tattoo around her breast. I prop up the pillows and sit down. She eyes my Styrofoam container. "I always liked *At Fillmore East.* What you got to eat?"

"I have no idea what you're talking about. It's a cheeseburger. Vegetarians don't eat cheeseburgers."

"I smell fries!"

D.H. and Alex are in his room. They've got the music up really loud, but it's The Spa Motel and nobody complains. They're fucking around, being silly, slam dancing between the two beds. The curtains are pulled back. The sliding glass picture window wide open. D.H. spins around, laughing manically. His arms are straight out. In his hand is an empty beer bottle. Without even thinking, he lets go of the bottle. It arcs out the window over the sidewalk and flies high above Lincoln Avenue. On the downward curve, it smashed against the windshield of a passing cop car.

The cop slams on his brakes. The screech of tires can be heard over the music. D.H. and Alex see the cops exiting their car and hurrying toward the motel, eyeing the open window to D.H.'s room the whole time. They tear ass out into the hallway, leaving the door wide open. In minutes, they're banging on my door. I let them in. They're out of breath laughing.

"Fucking cops. Beer bottle," is all the information I get.

When I hear "cops," I lock the deadbolt and tell them to chill. After they calm down, I get the whole story, but not before all my fries are eaten. "Fuckin' vegetarians." I hold my burger close in case any of them decide now is the time to covert to carnivore.

"Did they see you?"

"Oh yeah, looked right at us."

"I'll be right back." I don't look anything like D.H. or have bright red dyed hair like Alex. The cops won't mistake me for either of them. I hit the hallway and run into Greg Allman's crew.

"You sure this is where you lost it?"

"No, I ain't sure. If I was sure, then I'd know where I dropped it."

"Lose something?" I ask, knowing full well what they're looking for.

"Just looking for our rooms. Little lost is all."

We all get on the elevator. None of Allman's guys are small and it's crowded. When the door opens, there's two angry Chicago cops—one with a baton in his hands. They quickly scan the elevator and decide we're not D.H. or Alex. The good ol' boys are spooked and quickly exit the elevator with their eyes on the floor.

"Evening officers."

"Shut the fuck up." They push past me into the elevator.

I head to D.H.'s room and run into Carleson. "Did you know Greg Allman's staying here?"

"Fuck Greg Allman."

The cops thoroughly trashed D.H.'s room. They smashed the TV, broke all the empty beer bottles, ripped the bed apart, and squirted shampoo all over his clothes. I cautiously walk through the debris and close the window. I'm hoping they don't suddenly appear behind me. Back in my room, I tell them the coast is clear and they owe me an order of fries.

***

The WUST Radio Music Hall in Washington DC rocks. Government Issue and Morally Bankrupt are the openers. It's a packed full house and DC audiences are overly enthusiastic.

Biafra is on a mission. He's tired and pissed and berating the audience. Hitting the stage, he immediately complains of how smoke-filled the room is and then launches into, "Why don't we start off this show with some kind of a note of hope that the violence caused by misguided pseudo patriotic pigs is going to stop!"

The mostly adolescent male crowd pushes up to the stage and cheers. It's obvious most of them have no idea what Biafra is talking about. They just want to the first song to start so they can jump on stage and cause shit.

"Oh, a brave person threw a beer can from the back, oh hey."

Klaus and Ray strum their instruments, goading Biafra to start. But he's too far into preaching and ignores them.

"Phony patriotic rednecks are what's bringing our country down!"

When the band finally launches into "Nazi Punks Fuck Off" the audience erupts with fists in the air. The small stage is overrun and there's no room to move.

"Come on. Don't be so selfish. Get off!" Biafra shoves a punk who's been skanking back and forth across the stage forever.

Ron is in the middle of the mayhem, tossing kids and trying to keep them away from Ray's gear. I wade in and clear an area around Biafra. D.H.'s kick pedal breaks. I fix it. The stagedivers are endless. Klaus's mic stand gets bumped and the mic hits him in the face. I right the stand and push everyone away. D.H.'s kick breaks again. The drive chain for the kick pedal has come undone. We don't have a spare. I'm under D.H.'s snare while he continues to play. I get the chain back on and he's good to go but my ears are ringing.

"How many of you believe that winning is everything? It's the only thing?" Biafra is pacing the stage. "All those hands kind of scare me in a way. How corrupt can you get?"

When the band rips into "Bleed for Me," Biafra jumps into the audience. The crowd surges toward him. I grab the mic cord and keep tabs on Biafra, being held aloft over the brutal movement of bodies pushing and shoving. It's so hot—there's no air and hard to breath. The stage is slimy with beer and sweat and then Biafra gets dumped back on stage, "Good night!"

The show is over.

***

6AM, crossing the Georgia state line heading south into Florida. I've been driving since we loaded out of Atlanta at 1:30 this morning. I'm tired, got a slight buzz, and burned out from not sleeping for the last few nights. Humid, salty ocean air blows in through the open window. Shadows are starting to focus into shapes in the morning light and the scenery has changed. Instead of nondescript countryside and sprawling suburbs there's palm trees, rural dirt roads, and all the buildings are one story low.

I've never been to Florida. I'm thinking pink flamingos, women in bikinis, sandy beaches, and orange groves. I'm seeing mobile homes, boarded up businesses, liquor stores, and poverty. But what state really looks good from the highway? I'm sweating. But the warm breeze feels good after the cold November north. I take a gulp of tepid beer and wedge the can between my legs as a highway patrol pulls alongside. The cop looks like a stormtrooper. He's wearing one of those Mounty hats. I can see him checking us out. I could give a fuck. I'm driving the speed limit. I'm almost positive no one in the truck has any drugs and he didn't see me take a drink. It's probably the California plates, which are never good. To the rest of America, we're all weed smokers. I fucking hate weed. Nobody in this truck smokes that shit.

The cop speeds up, swerves into our lane a few car lengths ahead, pops his red light, and pulls over a rusted pickup truck held together with duct tape and baling wire. I ease up on the gas and change lanes to get around him, and head further south into the dawning light.

Everything alongside the highway has that beat up look. Sort of raggedy and used. Like a lot of the South, it appeals to a northern city boy like me. Shabby roadside business, trailer parks, fast food joints, and dark, windowless, neon-lit bars. There're strip clubs, liquor stores, Baptist churches, rebel flags, and pickup trucks with gun racks. It's like a third world country full of white folks.

Chris is in the passenger seat smoking a cigarette. Ron is sitting between us on an Anvil case. Anna Lisa and Alex are asleep in the back. After a month and a half on the road, Carleson finally bailed as tour manager. Now it's all on me. Ray is totally cool with it. He just wants me to be more proactive, call the venues, check on the PAs. More and more, we're getting promoters who misrepresent the sound gear and the show's quality suffers. But it's Biafra who isn't happy with me being road manager. In Atlanta, he introduced me as, "Our road manager by default," which didn't instill a lot of confidence. I'm worried I'll fuck something up and I'm second-guessing myself. I'm stressing about everything.

It's 9PM. We're at the Cameo Theater in Miami. The local punk scene is a little weird. Even though there's the usual hardcore leather jacket and spike-wearing punks, they're mixed with heavy metal kids sporting Iron Maiden T-shirts, pouty, white-faced goths, and your average thrill-seeking high school kids. It's not like these types of folks never come to our shows, but it's a much more varied and racially diverse crowd than usual. Not only are there white skinheads, but Black skinheads, Latino skinheads, and little girl skinheads with those weird bangs on the front of their bald heads. At the bar, there are longhaired bikers and a strange assortment of regular Joes, the kind you'd find at any diehard drinking establishment. On the fringe of the pit parental types watch their kids slam dance with expressions of abject horror.

It's one hundred degrees or more inside and half of the audience is wearing leather and spandex. I'm thinking stinky body odor. I'm thinking yeast infection. I'm thinking I've had twenty beers, sweating my ass off, and pissed only once in the last eight hours.

The crew and band are tired. We're all just trying to get through the night. Half passed out in the dressing room, I sleep through the raging sound of the Italian band, Raw Power. Louder than hell, they blow away the openers and then the Kennedys hit the stage. Biafra is in fine form. He's in the crowd, screaming the lyrics, his sweat flying. I spend most of the night untangling mic cords, shoving stagedivers, and drinking beer. A little girl slugs me in the head. Before I can react, she flips me off and jumps backwards into the crowd.

After the show, I get the band out the door, into cabs, and start packing up the gear. Load-out is in an alley behind the club. A dark BMW with half-lowered tinted windows slowly cruises by the truck. It's filled with tattooed thugs and rap music is blaring so loud the speakers sound blown. A group of street kids behind a dumpster are causing a scene. They're wasted like glue sniffers or paint huffers or maybe PCP freaks. They hover in the shadows and stumble around, bumping into each other and shouting incoherently.

The club owner has his guys shove our gear and boxes of T-shirts out the stage door before we're ready. We have a system to packing and usually take the gear out in that order. The alley is full of our stuff randomly piled around the truck. I'm going through it all to make sure nothing has been left behind. Without warning, the house crew pulls down graffiti-covered metal security grates on all the doors—the resounding crash of metal on concrete echoes in the night—then the locks are slammed shut and the lights go out. The glue sniffers are still there. The BMW is idling at the end of the alley. I'm tired and want to get out of here. We have a week off for Thanksgiving. The Kennedys are going home, and the crew is staying in Miami Beach.

We check into the hotel, a rundown ten story pink art deco building right on the beach. There's a forlorn, seedy look to the place. The lobby furniture is old and saggy. The walls are scarred from years of luggage carts passing through and the carpets are threadbare. We drop our bags with the front desk and tell them we'll be right back, just need to deal with the truck.

The hotel is on a main drag with old art deco buildings lining both sides of the street. Music blasts out of a basement club, but the sidewalk in front is empty. All the parking meters are broken, their metal casings hanging open and empty where the coins were stored. I'm surprised. This is Miami Beach, albeit South Miami Beach. I thought it was going to be more resort-like. Only, the neighborhood is sketchy. Groups of young thugs hide in the shadows openly drinking. I catch a man pulling on the padlock to the back of our truck. When I tell him to fuck off, he gives me the look of death.

I ask the doorman if there's somewhere safe to park the truck. He directs me to the rear of the building to a parking lot with a ten-foot chain link security fence, coils of concertina wire strewn across the top. Like a prison, or some border crossing. The doorman has a gun holstered to his belt.

"Damn, that's hard core," I say.

"Welcome to Miami," says Chris.

"It's hot," says Anna Lisa. "I wanna go swimming."

It's four in the morning—the temperature well over ninety degrees. A weird light, twilight and sunrise mixed, is creeping into the peripherals. In front of us stretches a huge, empty beach with a wood-planked walkway leading off into the night. In the distance, the huge hotels of Miami Beach jut up into the sky. I haven't slept in days, but I'm strangely not tired.

Anna Lisa takes off running toward the ocean. Chris and I follow her. She's got her clothes off, naked, jumping into the dark surf. I sit down and pull a warm can of beer from my jacket and light a cigarette. So does Chris. We drink as Anna Lisa swims.

"It's fuckin' beautiful," says Chris.

"Got a knife?" I ask.

He hands me a folded blade. I flip it open and cut my pants into shorts. I'm wearing motorcycle boots. There's only a foot of exposed skin between the top of my boots and the bottom of my cutoff pant leg. It feels goofy. But then Chris does it too and I don't feel as weird. We're drinking beer and laughing. Anna Lisa's in the surf, giggling and screaming. The waves crash around her and they're phosphorescent.

"Look!" she yells. "The water is fuckin' glowing."

"I'm on acid," says Chris and then laughs.

I glance his way, but don't ask. Chris has been known to drop acid. He once drove all night from Reno to Seattle through a torrential rainstorm totally frying and no one knew.

There's brightness out to sea and I realize it's the sunrise. I'm not used to the sun rising out of the ocean. I've been on the West Coast too long.

Yesterday, I was reading an article about Florida in *The New York Times*. An elderly couple was watching TV in their living room when a duffle bag full of cocaine crashed through the roof, almost killing them. Hundred pound bales of marijuana were washing up on shore. Drug cartels were running rampant. Gangs were having shootouts in broad daylight. The place sounded insane, and here we are sitting on Miami Beach at 5AM calmly watching the sunrise.

Anna Lisa's fresh out of the water, putting on clothes. Chris is checking her out, watching her get dressed. We're out of beer and cigarettes. It's time to go.

The back entrance to our hotel leads into a large area by a pool with lounge chairs and tables with umbrellas for shade. Which, at this time in the morning, except for a man setting up the bar of a thatched hut, is practically deserted.

"This is so cool." Anna Lisa lies down on a lounge chair.

The sun is still on the horizon. It's already a hundred degrees. Chris and I hit the bar.

"Buena mañana mis amigos." The bartender is dressed in black pants, white shirt, red vest, and bow tie. His hair is slicked back. He's got the coolest pointed black shoes. I'm standing here half naked, wondering how he's not drenched in sweat.

"Vodka tonic." I say.

"Whiskey sour," says Chris.

Two hours and a dozen drinks later we're still at the pool. Other hotel guests have come out and it's crowded. Calypso music plays in the background from speakers on poles. The bar is busy, but the area around us is strangely deserted. A pile of empty glasses and clothes lie next to our chairs. Anna Lisa is asleep. Chris is mumbling. I'm not really listening. I've got my shirt off, but my boots and cutoffs are still on. I think about ordering another drink. Instead, I roll over on my stomach and close my eyes.

I'm burning hot. My head hurts. I try to move and feel stiff. My throat is parched. I need something to drink. Chris is asleep in the lounge next to me. Anna Lisa is passed out next to him. The pool area is empty. There's no one at the bar. When I move, I feel like I'm on fire. The back of my legs, between the boots and the cutoffs, is glowing red and hot to the touch.

I sit up and look around. The sun is directly above us. It's fucking hot as hell. I shake Chris. "Man, what time is it?"

"Fuck." Chris is licking his lips and blinking in the sunlight.

I find my sunglasses, stand, and get dizzy. "Anna Lisa," I say and hold on to the back of a chair. "Anna Lisa," I say again. I feel like I'm yelling her name.

"Whaaa?" she says, raising her head.

"Let's go."

The lobby feels incredibly cold. It's a relief to get out of the sun. The desk clerk stares as we ask for our bags and room keys.

We're drunk, half naked, and disheveled—our clothes in disarrayed piles in our arms.

"I gave them to you last night," he says.

"Not us. That was the rest of our party. We have a suite and several other rooms."

The elevator screeches up nine flights. The door opens to a long, dark hallway. I find our room and open the door. The walls are yellow, the curtains thin and white. There's a slight moldy smell, mildew and rotting vegetation. I lie down and pass out on the bed.

If anyone looks Irish, it's me. I have a big blockhead and pale-ass skin with tons of freckles. I spend most of my time in dark clubs, and even then it's at night. I don't do sunshine or the great outdoors. The part of me that's even remotely tanned are my arms from hanging out the window when we drive, and that "tan" is really just a mass of large dark freckles with pink skin underneath. My best sleep is from 5AM to 12 noon. When I eat breakfast, it's usually at 4AM. I don't do mornings. I fucking hate the sunshine.

When I was a kid, maybe ten years old, my family was on vacation in Eastern Europe, which sounds a lot better than it was. Family vacations meant we all crammed into a Ford Cortina and drove backroads that were less traveled, stopped at decaying hotels and hostels, and pretty much roughed it. Hours and hours of us three kids staring out the window or at each other while our parents bickered. Yet, for some strange reason, my father decided we'd take a ferry to Pag, an island in the Asiatic Sea off what was then Yugoslavia. It was beautiful, sun swept, and washed out like a lot of the Mediterranean—but it was utilitarian and very Soviet—a worker's paradise getaway. My parents never took us to sunny beaches, so I was confused as to why we were there.

For two days we ran on the beach, went swimming, and hung out with a group of delinquent kids who were into drinking beer and smoking cigarettes—much like their parents. By the last night, I was totally sunburnt and taking a shower to cool down. Suddenly, I was freezing cold. I couldn't stop my teeth from chattering. The water felt warm. My body felt frozen. I started to pass out. My first time I experienced sunstroke.

I wake up and can't move. The sunburnt skin on the back of my legs is taut and burning to the touch. I can't remember the last time this part of my body has seen daylight. I light a cigarette, search my jacket pockets for pills, and there are none. I'm in fucking agony and don't have any drugs to kill the pain.

"We're all going out to the beach." Anna Lisa walks out of the bathroom. She's oblivious to my predicament. Fresh out of the shower, putting on her bikini. Anna Lisa tans. She's a golden brown, which totally fucking annoys me.

"Got any drugs?"

"Sleazy guy in the lobby offered me coke. Want me to get you some?"

I fucking hate coke. Who wants to be awake and jittery?

"Fuck you," I say and roll over. We have five days off and I can't even get out of bed. After a few minutes of feeling sorry for myself and staring at the wall, I grab the phone and call the front desk.

"Do you have room service?"

"Of course sir, let me connect you."

"Room service," says a heavily accented female voice, the sounds of a busy kitchen in the background.

"I need something strong to drink. Alcohol. I need it now."

***

Carleson maybe gone but her and Ken's booking still plagues us. We've shows back-to-back in multiple states and the pace is bone breaking. The week off in Miami helped, but we're all weary and a little testy. The promoter in Orlando screwed up the motel rooms and shorted us by one. Chris, Ron, and Alex complained they were all sharing one room. To avoid having to pull rank and press the issue, Anna Lisa and I slept in the truck.

More and more, Ron and Chris are angry about the slightest problem. I'm getting, "You're the road manger. You fix it." I can't count on either of them. I feel abandoned, like we're not even friends.

When I score dope in Montgomery, Alabama from a wannabe biker in a dark bar, Chris is the first to ask for a hit.

"You're the soundman, you score your own." I say and immediately regret it. "Look, man. I need you to back me up. Fuck Ron. He's pissed about the drugs. I can't do anything about that. But you're my best friend. Seriously, dude."

Chris and I have been tight friends for over seven years. We've toured and lived together. I give Chris a generous hit and we never talk about this again.

***

It's not a very good article. But who's really ever going to see it, as it's published in some obscure college student newspaper? I've got the paper in my hands and I'm trying to read as Biafra paces back and forth. He's woken me at eight in the morning. I don't do mornings unless I've been up all night. Apparently, Biafra *has* been up all night, stressing over this stupid article. Supposedly an interview of him that never took place.

I read the first sentence out loud. "Dressed in black leather and adorned with swastikas like a punk rock god, Jello Biafra descends from his tour bus."

Biafra stops pacing, "Adorned with swastikas. I'm not a Nazi. I don't wear leathers. I'm not in the Misfits. This is fucking ridiculous."

"Yeah, and we don't have a tour bus." I don't mention the punk rock god part, and, oddly, neither does Biafra. "So you never actually gave this interview?"

Biafra gets interviewed a lot. There's constantly some journalist or some nerd punk with a fanzine hanging round. I'm not sure Biafra actually knows whether or not he did or didn't get interviewed by this student reporter. Although the leather and swastika quote pretty much cinch the deal this kid never even laid eyes on him. Biafra's fashion sense is more blue jeans, work boots, and some horrid, unknown band's T-shirt. He'd rather be dead than caught wearing Nazi regalia. The only leather I've ever seen him wear is one of those disco jackets made of different colored leather bits sewn together, in a semi-sports coat that's got to be one of the ugliest pieces of clothing I've ever been forced to witness.

"No. I was never interviewed by that asshole. Fuck!"

Biafra is stressed out—way the fuck stressed out—and way more stressed out than necessary. It's just a lame article no one will read. If some kid hadn't shown it to him last night, he'd never known it existed.

"I want you to call them."

"Call who?"

"Call the newspaper. I want a retraction."

It's Saturday morning. We've got a show at a local club, and I'd like to get there sometime in the afternoon for soundcheck. Granted, I'd still be asleep if Biafra hadn't barged into my room screaming about this article. Spending my morning trying to get ahold of somebody at this student newspaper on a weekend doesn't sound that inviting. I'm figuring dealing with Biafra's shit comes with the "road manager by default" title. So, I search the masthead for a telephone number. Finding one, I press the digits on the motel room phone, then light a cigarette as it rings.

"Hello," says a voice on the other end of the line.

"Hi," I say, a little taken back someone actually answered. "This is Patrick O'Neil, road manager for Dead Kennedys. I'd like to talk with someone in charge about the article in your newspaper."

"Okay. I'm the editor. What can I do for you?"

"It's about this interview with Jello Biafra."

The guy laughingly snorts. "Yeah, what about it?"

Biafra is standing over me. He's actually shaking he's so worked up. I raise my hand palm up in an effort to pacify him. Instead he begins pacing again.

"We're not happy with the content. In fact, we're pretty sure your reporter never even interviewed Biafra."

"Is that so?"

"Yeah, that's so. Just whom am I speaking to?"

"I'm the editor."

"You don't have a name?"

"How do I even know you're really with the Dead Kennedys?"

"Because I just told you so. Who else would call about this article?"

"We get a lot of crackpots calling in, saying strange things."

"Okay editor who won't give me his name. How many people you got calling in saying your reporter is a goddamn liar? The person he says he interviewed never spoke with him? Do you know the definition of slander and what constitutes a libel suit?"

"Oh. Fuck. No," groans Biafra, and starts waving his hands. I cover the phone receiver and ask him what's wrong. "We're not some conglomerate music label with lawyers. Jesus Christ, don't say we're going to sue."

Obviously, Biafra's punk credentials are at risk here. I let this editor's fuckhead attitude get to me and blurted out the wrong thing. Only I'm not sure what else I could've said, or how to approach this.

"We have integrity. We stand by our reporters."

I'm thinking this newspaper's print run, at tops, is five hundred. How many people call about anything? How many people actually read this fucking rag? Who the hell does this editor think he is? Not like he's working for *The New York* fucking *Times*.

"We want a retraction." I say, and as the words come out of my mouth, I know how lame it must sound.

"We want it today," whispers Biafra, but loud enough for the guy to hear over the phone.

"A retraction? You want it today?"

"Yeah," I say. "We're playing in town tonight and we want you to make this right in print."

"We can't print an issue today. We're a monthly."

"You need to make this right. Or you'll leave us no other recourse than to force the issue."

Biafra stops pacing and groans. He's totally freaking out. I'm not handling this the way he wants. He wants me to be politically correct, and my style is more fuck you, I don't care, we're Dead Kennedys. But right now I'm all he's got.

Carleson quit mid-tour with another month of shows to go. I'm still resentful they hired her in the first place. It's not like I don't know the job. I originally thought Biafra didn't have any confidence in me. But over the course of this tour and the conversations we've had, I've come to realize it probably has more to do with my association with politically incorrect bands, meaning T.S.O.L. and Flipper. Plus, I'm a hotheaded drug addict prone to violence.

"Go ahead, force the issue," says the editor. But he sounds unsure of himself and after a few seconds of silence says, "I could maybe talk with the reporter and... if there were discrepancies... publish a statement in the next issue."

"Next issue?" I raise an eyebrow at Biafra, looking for his reaction.

"That's not soon enough," he mumbles. "I need something tonight."

I cover the receiver again. "It's the best we're going to get. What do you want me to tell him?"

"Hang up," says Biafra.

"We'll get back to you." I hang up the phone.

"I don't want people thinking I wear swastikas."

I light another cigarette and lean against the bed's headboard. I want to go back to sleep. I want to shoot some dope. I want a beer. I want a Valium. I want Biafra to get the fuck out of my room. But he sits down on a chair, his head in his hands, upset like he's going to cry. I wonder what it's like to be Biafra, and then I'm glad I'm not him. I just make tours happen. I don't have to perform. I don't have to deal with the fallout, the hype, and the bullshit.

I take another hit on my cigarette, blow out a smoke ring, and shut my eyes. I hear the door close as Biafra leaves.

2015. I'm on book tour for my memoir Gun, Needle, Spoon. *I'm reading at Book Passage in Marin County. It's a packed event and I'm stoked. Literary readings are hit or miss. They can be well attended or like the one in Boston where it was just my dad, Maya, Jae Johnson, Billy Jordan, Glen Stilphen, and a bag lady looking for entertainment. Not exactly glamorous, but then again, the majority of people in America don't read or buys books anymore. I'm grateful I'm not reading to an empty room.*

After the reading, as I'm signing books, a representative of a decent indie press asks if I'm interested in co-writing Biafra's memoir. I'm momentarily taken back and don't have an immediate response. I haven't seen Biafra in over ten years, and that was just running into him on the street in San Francisco, shooting the shit for a quick minute.

"How's your relationship with Jello?"

"I think it's good?"

There had been that whole lawsuit with the D.K.'s catalog due to mismanagement by Alternative Tentacles. The Kennedys were playing shows with a new lead singer and Biafra refused to ever be on stage with the band again. But I never had anything to do with any of that. There shouldn't be bad blood between Biafra and me.

"I'd have to get paid," I tell the guy. "I'm not a youngster working for free anymore. I'm a writer. This is how I make a living."

He says his publisher is going to run it by Biafra and then get back to me. I don't say it, but I'm worried writing someone else's memoir is going to interfere with my own work. I have this memoir and a novel I've already started. I don't really have time for another project.

I never hear from that guy again. I'm gathering Biafra didn't like the idea. Even though I was hesitant to commit to the project, there are still a lot of emotions attached to Dead Kennedys. It's like Biafra's inadvertently sending me another vote of no confidence and all the old resentments and fears from touring resurface again.

I fucking love New Orleans. If there's one city in America that knows how to have a good time, it's New Orleans. You drive through the South with all the blatant racism and Civil War history and hit New Orleans and it's a whole different world. Not that there aren't openly racist folks and the N.O.P.D. isn't known for shooting anyone that isn't white. But there's an unspoken agreement we're all here to party as hard as possible and damn everything else.

The promoter booked us into the Bayou Plaza Hotel, a sprawling two-story complex that was a holdover from better days. There was a dormant dinner theater in the back and the lobby was freakishly huge. We're early and the rooms haven't been cleaned, but the hotel manager is doing his best to accommodate us. I'm telling him to get the band their rooms first, the crew can wait, and he totally gets it.

Across the lobby there's a group of people lounging on sofas. They look cool, like musicians. They're also checking us out. Anna Lisa whispers, "That's Tom Waits."

"No shit?"

I sneak a quick glance. It's Waits and I'm pretty sure that's John Lurie, having seen the Lounge Lizards in New York years ago.

The rest I don't recognize, except there's a tall guy with a mane of gray, white hair and a blonde woman who both look familiar. Maybe Waits is playing tonight, which sort of sucks because we might lose some of our audience.

We find out many years later that it was Jim Jarmusch and company, and they were filming Down by Law. *Waits, never a big fan of punk rock, doesn't readily acknowledge us. Later we'll meet some of the film crew. A few ask to buy T-shirts. The next night, Alex and Anna Lisa run into Waits wandering the hallway with a bottle of champagne. He's talkative and friendly but they're too star struck to introduce themselves.*

The film will come out later that year. I'll be too strung-out to actually go into a theater and sit still long enough to watch a movie. I'll eventually see the film on video. Many years after that, Wait's former soundwoman Diane Franklin will introduce us at his daughter's art show in a Santa Monica gallery. Standing around outside away from the bar, neither of us drinking, I'll think it too lame and fanboy-ish to tell Waits about our "almost meeting" in New Orleans.

The 601 Club is downtown, right off the French Quarter. The promoter literally opens the bar to the crew and band. "Drinks are on the house. There's beer if you actually want to waste your time drinking that instead of hard liquor." Anna Lisa has this huge red drink. "It's a hurricane," she yells over the noise of the opening band. I take a sip. It's fruit punch and a ton of alcohol. I almost gag. Anna Lisa is already wasted, and the show has barely started.

The rest of the night is a blurred memory. A friend of my father's, a professor at Tulane, hangs out with us, and then we're in the French Quarter. We've all got drinks in big plastic "go cups" and we're hitting one club after another. It's the entire road crew and

Ray is with us. I think Klaus and D.H. are there for a minute and then they're gone. I don't know where Biafra is.

A bartender gives me a '50s tie. I am wearing a cut-off T-shirt so I find this a bit confusing. I stuff it in my pocket because it's kind of cool. In the same pocket are six odd, twisted plastic bindles of heroin and have no idea where I got them. Thankfully, I'm drunk enough to know I'd probably die if I shoot any of it. Only I'm not sure if I already have. We start collecting a following, bartenders and waitresses from the clubs we've closed, and a few punks from the show. We all end up at Johnny White's because it's open twenty-four hours. One of the waitresses in our group insists we all drink Jägermeister, an alcohol I've never heard of. It's served in shots, ice cold, and tastes like cough syrup. I don't remember what time we finally left the bar, but there was the hint of daylight.

I wake up in the cab of the truck. Ray is driving. Anna Lisa is passed out between us. It's sunny, way too bright, and I've got the worst headache I've ever had in my entire life. "Where are we Ray?"

"Trying to find the damn hotel."

The Bayou Plaza is at the intersection of Carrollton and Tulane Avenues. From the club, it's a straight shot down Tulane. Or if you take I-10, it's right off the Carrollton exit. It's almost 10AM. Ray has been driving for hours. We're on the elevated Pontchartrain Expressway. I can see the huge Bayou Plaza sign off to our left, but it's in the distance and getting smaller.

"It's over there, Ray."

"I know. I passed it three times already."

Ray and I are laughing our asses off. Anna Lisa wakes up and wants to know what's so fucking funny. We finally get off the expressway and pull into the parking lot. We've the day off, which is great as I'm incapable of going anywhere except my room to puke and then pass out. Fuck Jägermeister.

It's four in the afternoon and Anna Lisa and I are still in bed. To say I was hungover would be an understatement. I have never felt this bad from drinking in my entire drinking career. I'm pretty sure I have alcohol poisoning.

"We have to get up," says Anna Lisa, but she doesn't move. The air conditioning is on full blast. I'm freezing. But I can't stand up to turn it off. "Could you shut off the AC? I think I'm going to barf." We both groan. Then we laugh. My head hurts. I want to die.

"I'm not feeling well," says Anna Lisa.

"I'm not feeling well either. I'm dope sick and hung over."

"No, I mean something's wrong. I haven't felt right since New York."

***

Houston, Texas, another shithole in a long line of shitholes. On the outskirts of the city, we pass oil refinery after oil refinery belching gray smoke into the vast blue Texas sky. Traffic is bad and we're barely moving. We're playing a 2,200-capacity heavy metal club in the characterless wasteland of central Huston. I'm driving past one strip mall after another, trying to find the venue. It's at least eighty degrees with one hundred percent humidity. After New Orleans, this seems mild and almost welcoming, but the crew is hot, everyone is on edge, Anna Lisa is sick, and tempers are short.

After load-in, Anna Lisa and I take a cab to the nearest hospital. She's been throwing up all morning and I'm worried. Anna Lisa is not one to complain. If she says she's sick, then it's bad.

The triage nurse at the urgent care clinic takes one look at us and decides we're here to steal something or get prescribed drugs. She's giving Anna Lisa attitude. I'm starting to get pissed. I'm sure it doesn't help that we dress and talk differently than everyone else. Two skinny-ass punks in torn, black clothing, obviously not from Texas or anywhere else south of the Mason-Dixon line.

I step outside to smoke. Anna Lisa's in an examination room dressed in a hospital gown, still waiting for the doctor. At this rate, we're going to be here forever. Across the street is a bar and I head over to use the pay phone and call the club to let the crew know we'll probably be late. It's an early all-ages show. But in Texas that doesn't mean shit. The Kennedys will probably go on around 11 PM. I've time for at least a cocktail before I head back to the hospital.

I've had a few drinks and I'm drunk. I get up off my barstool to take a piss and a tall blonde cowgirl literally grabs my crotch outside the men's room. I'm taken back by her boldness, but I'm a little turned on as well. I'm thinking if she's not a hooker this could be interesting. Then I remember Anna Lisa's forlorn face when I left her.

The sun is setting as I exit the bar. I have no idea how long I've been drinking. I stumble off the curb and jaywalk against the light. Cars fly by, narrowly missing me, and honk their horns.

The triage nurse scowls at me from the reception desk as I cross the lobby. I'm close to telling her to eat shit but first I want to find out what's happening with Anna Lisa. In the examination room, a doctor and a nurse are standing over her, blocking my view. I ask what's going on and they turn to look at me. The nurse has an ultrasound probe on Anna Lisa's stomach. On the machine's monitor there's a grainy black and white image of a small fully formed fetus. Pulsing over a small set of speakers is a faint heartbeat. Anna Lisa's eyes are wide with abject horror or maybe impending guilt.

"What the fucks going on?" I grab Anna Lisa's hand. "You okay?"

"You the father?" The doctor is tall and white and very stern. He holds his hand out for me to shake. "Congratulations."

I look at his hand. I look at the nurse. Are these people living in an alternative universe? Do Anna Lisa and I look like quality parenting material? Both of them have the glow of zealot Christians.

They're scaring the shit out of Anna Lisa. Tears are running down her face. Her eyes are pleading with me.

"Did you want them to do this?" I gesture at the ultrasound machine.

"No," whispers Anna Lisa, pulling the hospital gown over her exposed stomach, hugging herself, and shifting away from the nurse. "They made me... listen... to the... heartbeat."

"Hon, your wife... well, wasn't sure she wanted the baby. I just wanted her to experience the joys of seeing a new life."

"Are you fucking kidding me?" I'm livid and swelling up as much as my 125 pound 5'10" junkie ass can swell. "You made her listen to the heartbeat? What the fuck is wrong with you people?" The doctor hurriedly leaves the examination room. The nurse stands her ground. She's an avid pro-lifer and no drug addict punk is going to intimidate her.

"Human life is sacred." The nurse crosses her arms and glares.

I have never actually met anyone who was openly anti-abortion before. The subject of children doesn't come up that often in the circles I travel in. None of the bands or road crew has kids. It's just not something we ever even considered or discussed.

Anna Lisa hurriedly dresses. I put my arm around her. "Don't worry. It's going to be okay." I'm nervous and wondering if that's actually true.

Anna Lisa is still crying as the cab pulls out of the parking lot. I have no idea what it's like to be a woman, let alone a pregnant woman. The guilt that nurse and doctor tried to pressure her with is unbearable to witness. I can only imagine how she's feeling.

Anna Lisa wipes the tears away. "I need to get loaded."

After the show, the whole crew is at a coffee shop sitting in a giant horseshoe-shaped booth with blue Naugahyde upholstery and gray Formica tabletop. It's 2AM. We're hungry. It's time for breakfast. We all order huge plates of food. There are stacks of pancakes, fried eggs, greasy grits, hash browns, cheese omelets, ham steaks, and crispy bacon. I'm pouring syrup on my pancakes and talking shit about grits. I fucking hate grits. "Why don't they just call them cream of wheat and serve them like oatmeal?" The local club owner is with us, and he argues that grits are different than cream of wheat, and either I don't know the beauty of grits or I've never had good grits. His words are slurred and he's talking really loud. I get self-conscious that the other customers will somehow weigh in on this grit argument and I let it go.

But the club owner keeps yammering on about the beauty of southern cuisine. He's sitting in the middle of the booth between Chris and me. He's got a piece of toast in his hand and a knife in the other. It looks like he's trying to play the violin, only his eyes roll back into his head and he starts drooling. Then he falls face first into his plate of food. Chris grabs the back of his collar and pulls him up. The dude is totally out of it, mumbling incoherently, his beloved grits dripping off of him. Chris slaps his face to tries and bring him back to life.

"I'm the fuckin' club owner!" he screams.

Everyone in the restaurant turns. The waitress scurries behind the counter and lifts the telephone. This is goddamn Texas. I'm pretty sure she's calling the cops. I've a pocket full of Valiums. Anna Lisa is carrying heroin. I have no idea what Chris is holding, but I'm sure it's a felony.

We grab the club owner from either side under the armpits and drag him backwards through the restaurant. "Our friend is really tired," I say to the dinning room full of customers. The waitress puts the phone down.

***

I have never played Mexico. It's just never been on any band itineraries. El Paso is about as close as we usually get, a stone's throw away across the Rio Grande. Our last show of the tour is at the Teatro de la Casa de la Cultura, in Tijuana. The promoter, Luis Güereña, meets us at the border and we sail through customs. I'm nervous about the drugs stashed behind the dashboard radio. But who smuggles heroin into Mexico?

We have lunch at a taco stand in a small plaza while waiting for the venue to open. We're eating fifteen-cent carne asada tacos, drinking cold Victoria beer, and everyone is tired but happy. At the nearest pharmacy I buy a box of generic methaqualone (Quaaludes) and a long strip of diazepam pills that look like candy and the pharmacist doesn't ask for a prescription. The federales drive by and wave. People are super nice. The punks are so stoked we're playing that they practically unload the truck for us.

The venue is incredibly dark. There's an intense anarchistic feel to the night. The bands are loud. It's rumored the cops are waiting to arrest us when the show ends, which turns out to not be true.

The night is hot, the air is still, and there's a sweet smell of jungle rot or maybe it's just garbage in the air. We all stop off at the local cantina. The margaritas are cheap and we're treated like punk rock royalty.

I'm laughing with everyone at the bar. Chris and Ron are joking around. Ray and Klaus are drinking with us. It's been a grueling three months and we're all letting off steam. I sit down at a table with a pitcher of margaritas with Anna Lisa, Rebecca Stafford, and two guys named Bill. A man who works for the bar wants to take our photo. It's one of those souvenir deals for tourists. We all hold our drinks up and smile. I'm actually happy.

I never want to stop touring. This is the most amazing life. Better than I could ever imagine. I don't have to deal with the normal shit that everyone else contends with. I'm constantly moving.

I never have time to actually consider how strung-out and messed up I really am. I can justify every bad decision. I can ignore reality. I'm on tour. Nothing can touch me.

WE'VE GOT A BIGGER PROBLEM NOW
1986: DEAD KENNEDYS

I leap off stage into the audience and land in a tight circle of drunk jocks and shit-faced college students. These aren't punks, just rowdy types looking to cause shit and kick some ass. Biafra's down, he's on the floor. A large jock in a UC Davis Aggies T-shirt moves in to kick him. I clock the motherfucker in the head and push backwards against the crowd behind me—clearing space. Ron is doing the same, making more room. The crowd surges to the left and then David Labrava is shoving his way into the clearing. Former Golden Gloves, future Hells Angel, future actor playing Happy on the *Sons of Anarchy,* David is someone you want by your side when the shit jumps off.

The promoter, Stewart Katz, had erroneously allowed UC Davis to use their school's wrestling team as security—fucking testosterone-fueled, muscle-bound, brain dead athletic majors with no experience working punk shows. It's a nightmare and Biafra has done his trademark stage dive into the audience. Usually they hold him aloft above their heads and I stay on stage with a sixty-foot mic cord, feeding it out and keeping tabs on him—trolling for Biafra— but Biafra picked the wrong section, or maybe he didn't. He landed on the jocks, and the jocks want to kill him. I see a normal-looking college kid slug Biafra in the side of his head. Biafra struggles before slipping down into the crowd, lost beneath a sea of people, and that's when I jump in.

We're playing UC Davis's Freeborn Hall. Which sounds like Lynyrd Skynyrd's "Free Bird" (hold your lighter in the air—rock on!) and I keep thinking we're at Chico State, but it's UC Davis. I'm so fucking confused. Only it really doesn't matter where we are. It's just another show, in a long line of shows, years of shows really, and once again I'm in the audience shoving people around.

The openers: Phranc, 7 Seconds, and Mojo Nixon, all kick ass. Target Video is on stage and in the audience shooting with three cameras and recording off their own soundboard. It's the D.K.'s swan song. This is the ultimate documentation of the band. The show is sold out, 2000 college kids in the San Joaquin Valley, halfway to Sacramento: farmland, small towns, 4-H clubs, and truck stops. Where agriculture is king. But the strip malls are encroaching.

I hate the fucking valley.

Ron yanks Biafra off the floor and directs him toward the stage. The mic is still there and I dive for it. The crowd pushes forward, filling the open space. I grab the mic cord and pull. Bodies fly in opposite directions. David's got my back. Ron's shoving Biafra onto the stage. I hoist myself up and hand the mic to Biafra. He stands at the edge of the stage and starts singing, the band of course having never stopped playing. Some moron kid grabs Biafra's leg and pulls. Biafra kicks and his foot connects. The kid goes down.

I walk over to my usual place behind the amps. A couple wrestlers are laughing and pointing at people in the crowd. I grab my beer and take a drink. The wrestlers notice me. The taller one says something. I can't hear him and say, "What?" He leans in and tells me he's security and I have to get off the stage. I tell him I work for the band. He reaches over and grabs my shoulder. I smack his hand away and take another drink from my beer. The motherfucker has a big shit-eating grin on his face and tries to grab my arm.

"Don't put your fucking hands on me."

We just stare at each other. Dude goes to grab me again. I shove him and he nearly falls but regains his balance. He's got this bemused expression on his face, like he knows he can kick my ass. I'm shorter and at least fifty pounds lighter. My junkie arms are thin. I'm strung-out, tired, and covered in sweat—and I know I can kick his ass, even if that's just the heroin talking.

Ray appears beside me. He's stopped playing and he's yelling at the wrestlers. Telling them to calm down, I work for the band, they need to do their jobs, and leave me alone. They look at Ray like he's speaking Swahili. But even lame ass guys like these can see he's in the band and knows what he's talking about.

Earlier in the day I'd driven up from San Francisco with Microwave and Anna Lisa in the D.K.'s van. Micro and I are talking crew logistics. There's going to be two soundboards: one for video, one for the house PA. We should've hired Chris to run the house, and Microwave could have done the video, but nobody thought of it, and Chris is in L.A. Ron and I will be working stage, and we're all lugging gear. Anna Lisa's along for the ride, and I'm expecting David to be there. I just don't feel like we've enough crew and regret not bringing someone else.

The sound is extreme. The PA is being redlined. The band is tight. D.H. and Klaus are in that space they get where they can't miss. Ray's a calculated mass of distorted notes, an Echoplex free for all, and Biafra is Biafra—all over the stage and in the audience's face. The crowd is in a frenzy, shit is flying, kids are stagediving, security is going apeshit crazy. It's a normal show for us—possibly scary and exotic for the rest of them.

And then it's over.

I'm in the dressing room checking for any stray gear that needs to be packed out to the van, and if there's still beer to take with us. A group of cops, uniformed campus police, and a few of the concert security guys show up in force in the dressing room. Our shows can be crazy, occasionally there's opposition: outraged communities, bomb scares, protesting parental groups. But that aside, we usually play the show and then leave. Police in the dressing room is not a common sight.

One of the cops points to me.

"Can I help you?" I ask.

"You Jello Biafra?" He's a big white guy—another farmer's son going rogue, leaving the family business for a bright future in law enforcement.

I'm thinking this can't be good. Biafra and I are roughly the same height and build. I might be a bit skinner, but we're both pasty-face white guys with short hair.

"Yeah, I'm Jello," I say.

"Nah, he's not Jello," says one of the asshole security guys.

"No, really. I'm Jello. What's this about?"

"We need to speak with you regarding an assault charge," says one of the real cops.

"Assault?"

"You sure you're Jello?"

Biafra walks into the dressing room. I shift my eyes sideways at him, hold my hand up, and then turn back to the cops.

"Mr. Biafra, you need to come with us," says a campus cop.

"He's not Biafra," says Biafra. "I'm Biafra."

The cops look at me, then Biafra. They all turn their heads in unison, trying to figure out who's lying. I break eye contact, shake my head, and think what a jerk Biafra is. If I'd gotten them to take me, we could have possibly used that as a defense, false arrest, all us punks look alike.

"Nice try," says the big white cop as he pulls out handcuffs. Then they're leading Biafra away. He's got this surprised expression on his face, like this can't be happening.

"We'll find out where they're taking you," Microwave calls out. "We'll get someone down there."

Biafra had kicked out the front teeth of the kid who'd grabbed his leg during the show. No one had even really seen it, but me. It was just a quick burst of movement, a swift kick, really just a reflex reaction. But, the kid's front teeth were missing, and he'd gone to the police, pressed assault charges, and now they were here. You can't really fault Biafra. The audience was hostile and he was still leery from getting hurt two years earlier at the Olympic Auditorium in L.A. After that incident, Chris had given Biafra a pair of lace-up steel-toed shoes, sort of semi-protection on stage that Biafra then always wore. It was those shoes that had knocked out the kid's teeth. Now Biafra was charged with assault.

We finish loading the van. It's cold, there's tule fog—dense fog in the valley that hangs three feet above the ground, and you can't see shit. No one is talking. We're exhausted. The band is gone. Biafra is in jail. It's time to go.

This was Dead Kennedys last show as the original band. Ray and Biafra's relationship had gone from bad to worse. We had just played two nights at the Stone in Berkeley, and then this show at UC Davis. There was no forewarning before the call from Ray. Dead Kennedys were calling it quits. I never tour with them again.

CLAMPDOWN
1986: ALTERNATIVE TENTACLES

It's 10AM. I'm late getting to work, and I have to stop to pick up Alternative Tentacles' mail. The post office is crowded. It's taking forever. I didn't have money for the parking meter, and I'm worried the van will get a ticket.

As usual, there are two large mailbags waiting for me. Every punk in the entire universe sends Biafra mail. To them, he's the punk messiah. Half our mail is mushy fan letters he'll actually read and trinkets he'll cherish. The rest are orders for records and merchandise.

"Goddamn punk kids," I mumble as I drag the bulging bags across the marble floors and out the polished brass and glass doors of this ornate public building.

A meter maid is circling the van, peering in the window, trying to spy the VIN number off the dash so she can write a ticket.

"Hey!" I yell, running towards her, dragging the bags behind me.

"I already started writing the ticket."

"You can stop any time." I toss the bags in the side door.

She walks to the back of the van, hastily jotting down the license plate. I take off, tires screeching.

"Fuck yoooou!" I yell out the window and flip her off for good measure.

Traffic is light. One thing about being late is I miss the morning commuters. I take an illegal left off Mission onto Eighth and head toward the office. I'm a regular working stiff now. The tours are over. The Kennedys broke up right before we were supposed to tour Brazil and Japan, which really pissed me off. I'd been scheduled for malaria shots and was brushing up on Yakuza tattoos. T.S.O.L. is in disarray, Subhumans haven't come back to America, and Flipper, without Will, is doing shit all nothing. With no income to pay rent and two major drug habits, I start working at Alternative Tentacles as the art department. I'm doing layouts for album covers, ads, and posters, and generally just hanging out for a little over minimum wage.

It's sort of strange coming into work every day. I still haven't come to grips with who I think I am as opposed to who I really am. So much of my self-image was wrapped up in touring and working with bands. I feel like I've lost something. I've gone from the road manager who makes tours happen to that guy who stands in line with all the other civilians. Then again, I'm strung-out and a total mess. No one else would actually hire me.

But working in the record business isn't that bad. I can still say I work in the music industry and leave my inflated ego somewhat intact. I get to work with Winston Smith. I drew the lettering for his *Bedtime for Democracy* cover. When I'm broke between paychecks—which is all the time—I pilfer petty cash, or steal mail, or a small stack of records to sell. So, there are perks.

Of course, AT being an "alternative work environment," everyone does several jobs. I pick up the mail every morning on my way to work. Only I'm always late and Microwave and Debbie give me loads of shit. But what they don't know is I have to score dope, shoot it, then get to work, and some mornings just take longer.

I pull the van into Rodgers Alley and drive to the warehouse's roll-up door. We share the space with Ruth Schwartz's Mordam Records, and Leslie Jambor's Black Wave T-shirt printing.

It's like some punk rock collective, only we're not that organized. With the door up, I back in the van. I grab my bag, leather jacket, the mail sacks, and I head into the office—a small walled-in area in the middle of the warehouse that houses the AT staff.

"You're late," says Micro.

I don't even answer. What's the point? I'm always late. His statement is rather rhetorical. I drop the mailbags at Debbie Gordon's feet. She looks up and rolls her eyes. Debbie is always rolling her fucking eyes and I'm not sure if it's because I'm late, that Micro even bothered to say something, or that there's the usual ton of mail.

I slip my bag off my shoulder onto the back of my chair and carefully cover it with my leather jacket. Lately, I've been scoring dope in a particularly nasty housing project off Potrero Hill, a few blocks from where I live. Even though it's easy to get in and buy the dope, getting out can be a bit of problem. All the local junkies wait in the shadows and stairwells to rip me off. As a precaution, I've been carrying an old .38 that I'm hoping works. But, I've never actually fired the damn thing. All I want the gun to do is scare the hell out of the other dope fiends so I can get back to the van and do my shot in peace.

Still, I'd rather not have everyone aware I've a gun, needle, spoon, so I always hide it in my bag under my jacket. Truth is everyone knows I'm strung-out. I'm not fooling anybody. Even though I act like I am. I just never come right out and said, "Hey, I'm a junkie," which causes a lot of tension. Leslie in particular is always mad at me. Angry at what I get away with. Debbie tolerates me, and knows I'm totally irresponsible, but laughs at all my jokes. Microwave just accepts this is who I am.

"You live in a barn?" says Micro.

"Fuck."

I walk out the office, past Ruth, who's always out there counting records, across the warehouse, and pull down the roll-up door. It's San Francisco. No matter the season the warehouse is freezing cold. Leaving the door open lets in a wind that chills to the bone. With a shitload of heroin in me, I can't feel the cold. But the days when I haven't been able to score and I'm waiting for Anna Lisa to bring me something, I huddle in the corner, my teeth chattering.

"What's on the agenda?" asks Micro when I return to the office.

"I thought maybe I'd smoke a cigarette."

"I need an ad for *Maximum Rocknroll*."

"I'll get right on it boss man."

The next hour I'm cutting and pasting a sloppy layout for an ad, sufficiently punk enough in its execution to look the part. The usual office small talk ensues: what band someone just saw, whose doing what with whom, where and what are we going to eat for lunch.

It's just Debbie and me in the office when Microwave calls out. "Debbie, Patrick, come out here." Micro sounds really formal and stiff, which is unusual and weird.

"What the fuck for?"

"Just come out here."

We walk out into what seems like a million cops, some in plain clothes. A few have guns in their hands.

"Sit," says a woman cop in uniform, indicating the couch and easy chairs in the area out front of the office.

"Where are the guns and drugs?" barks a plainclothes cop. A gold shield hangs from a chain around his neck.

Fuck. I'm thinking of the meter maid, the fuck you, and driving off burning rubber. But, I quickly discard that thought. There are too many damn cops for that to be the reason they're here. This is for something much more serious.

"There's no guns and drugs," says Microwave.

Except there is. In my bag. Under my jacket. On the back of my chair. Right in front of the ad layout I'm working on. It's not going to take a rocket scientist to figure out whose shit that is. I'm starting to get nervous. I want to take the Xanax I have in my pocket. Then realize, I have a fucking Xanax in my pocket.

I take a nervous glance at all my co-workers and know I'm putting them all in danger. Alternative Tentacles is not a hot bed for illegal firearms or drug sales. In fact, I'm the only drug addict and the only one with a gun. For the cops to even be there is totally ludicrous and thoroughly indicative of how the authorities really view punks and our music.

"Can I get a smoke?" I ask the room full of cops.

"No."

"What's this all about?" asks Microwave.

The cops are being evasive. There's a couple of detectives from Los Angeles, some Feds in suits, one in a weird uniform I can't figure out, a group of San Francisco detectives, and a bunch of uniformed S.F.P.D. While the detectives are busy in the office searching through drawers and shelves, the others keep us sitting and ask questions. The detective with the gold shield hanging from his neck starts taking notes. The other detective asks everyone their names and what their job is. The Fed holds his hand out and asks for our IDs.

"You work here?" he asks me.

"Yeah."

"Doing what?" he says and looks at my driver's license. "Mr. O'Neil?"

"I'm an artist. I'm the art department."

"Artist? You draw posters?"

"I've done some posters."

One of the cops comes rushing out of the office. "We've got it!" He has an expression on his face like he just came in his pants.

My heart jumps into my throat. I start sweating. My stomach turns. I'm expecting him to have my bag. Instead, he's holding a handful of negatives. The kind used for printing. Halftones for color separation.

The cops get all excited and go into a huddle.

"I really need a cigarette," says Debbie. "Can I get my pack in the office?"

The woman cop in uniform gets the okay nod from the detectives and follows Debbie while she retrieves her smokes. When she sits down, we all grab one and light up in unison. Holding the lighter, I notice my hand is shaking.

The cop with the gold badge breaks from the huddle and walks over to me. "You ever go by the name Giger?"

"Dude, I'm not Giger. Giger's famous. He lives in Sweden." Actually, I'm not sure where the hell Giger lives. Although, it's rumored he lives in a brothel in Sweden. But who the fuck really cares?

"So you didn't draw this?" Holding up the halftone negative for the *Frankenchrist* poster—the Giger drawing "Penis Landscape" with Winston Smith's red, white, and blue, D.K. logo border.

"Fuck no."

The cops are packing up posters, negatives, and halftone color separations into several boxes.

"Are we under arrest?" asks Microwave.

"No."

"We're free to go?"

"No."

The main cop, an SFPD detective, is on his radio. He's talking to some higher up, and it sounds like they're coordinating another raid. "Okay, it's a go," he says to one of the plainclothes cops.

The entire cop entourage gleefully shuffles out the front door. I jump up and run into the office. My chair is right where I left it, the jacket still discreetly coving my bag.

Back out in the lounge area everyone is still sitting around in shock. No matter A.T.'s reputation, we're not some smoking bed of anarchy. This the first and only time we've been raided.

"I gotta hit the bathroom," says Debbie.

"I'll go with you." I'm nervous and just want to get the fuck out of there.

Across town the cops are storming Biafra's home—a two-story house in the Mission district with a heavily overgrown yard. Every inch of his house is packed with stuff: records, posters, Dead Kennedy and Winston Smith artwork, framed and on the wall. Cut out and taped to his refrigerator are milk carton ads for missing children, "Have you seen this child?" The cops take a special interest in these ads—what kind of sicko has missing kids on his kitchen fridge?

A teenage girl bought *Frankenchrist* for her younger brother. The boy opened the record, in front of their parents, and pulled out the poster—and the wallpaper-like repeating image of crusty erect cocks inserting into equally grungy vaginas suddenly invaded their lives. The mother was shocked. Shocked enough to call the cops. The Los Angeles City Attorney's Office charged Biafra and Microwave with "distributing harmful material to a minor" and brought them to trial. A year later the jury became deadlocked, and the judge declared a mistrial.

A year later and I'm so strung-out I can no longer make it in to work at Alternative Tentacles. On one of the days I actually do go into the office, I get into an argument with Leslie, and she calls me a junkie. Pissed off at being accused of using drugs, I storm out of the office and never return. Debbie has to retrieve the D.K.'s van I drove home and parked in front of my house. Less than two months later, Anna Lisa attempts suicide and enters rehab. I eventually leave San Francisco for New York to clean up. After a year of drinking myself to death, but staying somewhat clean off heroin, I return to California and move to Los Angeles.

SO MESSED UP
1991: LOLLAPALOOZA

I'm starving. My stomach is growling. It's Saturday. I've spent the day at a huge Culver Studios' sound stage loading in for rehearsals and setting up the Lollapalooza Tour. It's the brainchild of Perry Farrell, Jane's Addiction's front man. The touring lineup is Jane's Addiction, Siouxsie and the Banshees, Living Colour, Nine Inch Nails, Violent Femmes, Fishbone, Ice T & Body Count, Butthole Surfers, and Rollins Band.

The immense stage and lighting tresses have been set up in the middle of this huge indoor space. Some of the bands have loaded in. Everyone is scheduled to sound check and work out their lighting. I'm on stage, knee deep in props. The idea is to have the entire stage look like a Mexican cantina, or maybe a Santería altar, complete with giant voodoo dolls hanging above the stage. I have been lugging all this stuff around for a friend of Perry's who is the "props manager" or "stage dresser" or some fucking title I've never heard of and really don't give a shit. He's setting it up for the first time and isn't too sure where everything goes. There're lights, piñatas, religious statutes, flowers, wreaths—a whole bunch a shit—and he wants it here, then there. Saying, "Nah, pile it up on the other side of the stage." I want to throttle him, or lay down and die, or both.

D.H. from Dead Kennedys is also working this gig, which is weird. D.H. doesn't normally work shows, or rehearsals, or stage, or anything. He's another friend of Perry's and Dead Kennedys no longer exist—so maybe it isn't weird. I owe D.H. a couple thousand dollars. Money loaned to rent a bungalow next to his in Hollywood. With my drug habit and lack of work and my drug habit adding to my lack of work, I haven't been able to pay him back—and working side by side is a little awkward, to say the least. But what is "good" is we're both strung-out and this morning on the way to rehearsal we've scored and are not only well, but definitely high.

I'm holding a large stuffed armadillo while the props manager loads a bank of votive candles onto the altar. An immense nod is creeping up my spine and I can feel my eyelids fluttering as I try to stay conscious.

"Dude, I'll be right back," I say and put the armadillo down.

"Don't be too long. Need help hanging the voodoo dolls."

"I can hardly wait."

I'm walking away when D.H. catches up with me. "Where ya going, Slick?"

"Gotta find something to eat. I'm fuckin' starving."

"There's vending machines across the way." The crew manager vaguely points towards the exit. He's a really nice guy. We'd met at another show where I'd been hired to load the sound gear and lighting. He had been the stage manager and that show had been a nightmare. I'd worked my ass off for very little pay. To make up for it, he'd called me in for this gig. The way he's been talking I'm thinking I've got a spot on this tour as a stagehand, which would be amazing.

"Cool. Thanks," I say, and D.H. and I head out the door.

Outside there are endless rows of giant white, windowless soundstages. Tucked into a smaller building on the corner, there's a small snack shop with several tables and chairs. The place is deserted. Either there's nothing going on, or everyone is busy working. Standing in front of the vending machine, I search my pockets for change. I've a dollar's worth and put the coins in the slot and press the button for a Snickers bar.

It's one of those machines where the candy bars and bags of chips are placed in coils that revolve, pushing the product to the front where it drops down and you retrieve it through a door at the bottom.

My Snickers starts moving and then stops right before being released. I bang the machine, but the Snickers doesn't move. I shake the machine. Still, the candy bar sits, just on the edge of the abyss.

"You got any change?" I ask D.H.

"Naw," he says, his hands held out empty.

"Fuck!" I grab the machine on both sides and start shaking it. When nothing happens, I grab it by the top and tilt it forward.

"Here, help me."

D.H. and I each take hold of the vending machine and pull down, lifting it up on its front bottom corner. The Snickers bar falls. So does a bag of Fritos.

"Hold on," I say. "Don't let it down yet. Okay, shake it."

We shake the machine, and bunch of chips and candy bars fall forward.

"Hey gents?" The crew manager is standing in the doorway of the snack shop. "Props manager needs ya. Ah... you probably shouldn't be doing that." He's got his head in the door, but his body is still outside, like he doesn't want to be mistaken as part of what we're doing. I've got my arms around the vending machine that's still poised in midair as D.H. holds it from the side.

The crew manager says, "Okay now," and then turns to leave.

"Be right there," I say.

We let the machine down. I scoop out bags of chips and a couple candy bars. So does D.H.

"That wasn't good," says D.H.

"You mean him seeing us robbing the vending machine?"

"Ah... yeah."

Back up on stage, the props manager has me holding a framed velvet painting of Our Lady of Guadalupe.

"Wha-da-ya think?" he asks.

"Think I gotta rest."

I put the painting down, wander backstage, find a pile of scrim and lay down. The dope is still working. I'm tired. It's hot. I'm coming down hard off the carbs and sugar. I want to take a short nap.

I wake up to a barrage of loud music noise. There's a woman screeching through the PA. My mouth is dry. I need a cigarette. I stumble out from backstage. A band is set up on stage and they're playing. I obviously missed load-in. There's a whole lot of gear and roadies setting up drum kits and tuning guitars.

"Who's this?" I ask the crew manager.

He looks me over and doesn't answer. Then shakes his head.

On the table off to the side of the stage there are cases of Coke and beer and a stack of pizzas. I walk over, grab a beer, and drink half.

"Those are for the bands." A guy I've never seen before is standing with a goddamn clipboard.

More and more road crews are being run by assholes with clipboards. The days of DIY punk tours are slipping away. It's as if we've gone full circle and we're back to the mega-rock arena shows that punk originally rebelled against. Every inch of me wants to act out and scream *We've lost our way*. I feel entitled to tell these clipboard-holding/headset-wearing techies how they're fucking punk up by making it corporate. I want to say, "I used to work for Dead Kennedys," and then realize just how sadly lame that sounds.

I finish the beer. Toss the can. Grab a slice of pizza. The guy looks at me like he's going to do something. I bang my shoulder into his as I walk past.

He calls me a fucking asshole and runs to the crew manager.

I hang with D.H. by the soundboard until the crew manager calls me over. Points to the road cases. Asks if I could tidy up a bit and stack the cases and gear they're not using out of the way somewhere. I move a couple cases, then light a cigarette and talk with a dude I know who works for another production company that has hired me on occasion.

The band finishes playing. The crew manager motions me over. "We're calling it a night," he says. "Here's your check. You can go."

I stare at the envelope in his hand. If I were going on tour, I wouldn't be getting paid tonight. It would be added on to my weekly check.

"What's this?"

"It's your pay. Thanks."

"I've a spot on the tour, right?"

"Well, we're looking for someone. But it's not you."

"Hey, if it's that thing with the vending machines..."

"No. It's more than that."

"Meaning?"

"You're just not right for the crew."

"But you called me in."

I know. And now I'm telling you no."

"Fuck." I take the envelope.

I find D.H., tell him I want to go, and if he wants a ride he'd better come with me. He's talking to a vaguely familiar looking dude. They're laughing and it bugs me they're having a good time. It's ten o'clock. I'm hoping a check cashing place is still open. If there is, and I cash this check, I can score on my way home.

"I just got canned," I tell D.H.

"What happened?"

"Don't know. Let's get outta here."

I never work in the music industry again. I'm too strung-out and I just don't care about anything except heroin. Eventually, I slip into committing small crimes and selling drugs. When Chris Grayson gets murdered during a drug deal, I numb out even more and my addiction becomes even worse. To pay for my habit, I start robbing drug dealers at gunpoint. I'm out of control and in the crosshairs of the L.A.P.D.

In fear of getting killed or incarcerated, I move back to San Francisco. I vow to kick heroin and get my life back on track. Unable to get clean, I end up shooting speed. After a year of insanity and no sleep, I meet Gina. She and I become a couple, get hooked on heroin, and try to navigate the world together. Only, we're two junkies and there's nowhere to go except deeper into our addiction. I can't keep us well middle-manning drugs deals and shoplifting. I turn to armed robbery.

IF I SHOULD FALL FROM GRACE WITH GOD
1998: SAN FRANCISCO COUNTY JAIL

"O'Neil," yells the deputy. "Got a visit."

It's Saturday morning in county jail. The usual audio overload of a hundred voices talking and yelling at the same time doesn't assault my ears. On the weekends, they let everyone sleep in. There's no work detail. No mandatory education groups. No nothing. I'm annoyed at being woken up. I'm wondering who the hell could be visiting. It can't be my mother. She was here last week. Nobody else bothers to come down and go through the hassle the deputies put them through just for forty minutes of staring at me through a two-inch-thick unbreakable window.

"Who is it?"

"They don't tell me, numb-nuts. Want the visit or not?"

"Fuck. Hold on. I'm coming."

June 25th, 1997, I was busted for multiple counts of armed robbery. I'd been robbing banks and local businesses for heroin money. I was totally strung-out and the daily cost of both Gina and my drug habit had become too much to bear. I was so loaded when I pulled my last robbery I barely got away. Two hours later, S.F.P.D. kicked in my door, arrested me, and took me down to central booking at 850 Bryant. I was charged with multiple counts of armed robbery. The cops called the Feds in case they wanted to prosecute me for the bank robberies. The Feds decided to pass when they learned the State of California was planning on seeking a Three Strikes, twenty-five-to-life sentence.

At my arraignment, the judge revealed the chilling news—the DA was gunning for me, and a Three Strike sentence was on the agenda. I blurted out, "Are you fucking kidding me?"

The entire following year, I sat in county jail twiddling my thumbs and occasionally getting arraigned on more robbery charges. The cops were clearing their books of unsolved bank robberies that fit my M.O. Truth is, I did do most of them. All these new charges gave my lawyer no leverage for a better plea bargain and the prosecutor's offers were just variations of the same deal. I waited out the ensuing legal battle reading books and writing in my cell. My life as I knew it was over. I wasn't going anywhere for the immediate foreseeable future.

I put on my shoes, leave the cell, and cross the dayroom. The guard is waiting at the sally port to the main corridor. The overhead lighting is glaring and, unlike the cellblock, the walls and floors are pristine clean. My work detail waxes and polishes these floors at night. We use so much liquid wax they almost glow. There really isn't shit all else to do in jail except this type of "make work." My reality consists of endlessly running a buffing machine all night while dreaming of someday getting out of here.

"Turn around." The deputy cuffs my hands behind my back and follows me as I walk down the hall. At the next barred gate, he hands me off to another deputy who un-cuffs me. I enter the visiting room rubbing my wrists. It's a long, cramped room, really a hallway. A low counter runs along one side, with stools attached to the floor in front of each window. The glass is so thick you need to use the phones on both sides of the windows to talk. There are ten other dudes from different cellblocks already in the room, all dressed in orange and shouting the usual jailhouse crap. It's annoying as fuck. But I'm used to it.

I sit at the only vacant stool and try to think who could possibly be here to visit me. I know it's not my lawyer. We only meet in the corridor outside the holding cell whenever I'm in court. Everyone else on the outside who's still speaking to me has already visited. Most never come back a second time.

I'm on the first window, which is the most undesirable as it's next to the guard and he can hear every word I say. On the other side of the glass is the entrance to the visiting room. The door opens and the room starts filling up as people begin filing in. There's a look of confusion on their faces as they pass each window, searching for the man they've come to visit. A pretty woman smiles, I notice she's pregnant, and watch to see which one of my fellow criminals she's here to visit. When I turn back to the window, Microwave, Winston Smith, and East Bay Ray are all standing there with big shit-eating grins.

I haven't seen these guys in years. It's a bit of a shock. Last time we were all together seems so alien and long ago—another world, another lifetime. I feel lightheaded. I reach for the phone. My gut twists as the anxiety kicks in. I'm embarrassed to have them see me like this—dressed in orange and on my way to prison. My hard jailhouse façade unravels. I hold back tears.

"Hey man," I say into the phone. "Good to see you guys."

THE END
2001: SAN FRANCISCO

I head out of rehab with my buddy, George. We got a pass to go to an AA meeting. We have to be back no later than midnight or get kicked out. Instead of following the rules, we're on our way to a Dead Kennedys show.

After eighteen months in county jail, my lawyer finally landed me a plea deal. The DA had gotten tired of dealing with my case. When they came at me with two strikes, time served, plus two years in prison, I take it.

When I get out, I don't have anywhere to live. I'm afraid I'm going to return to shooting dope. Catch another felony. Then definitely land in prison for the rest of my life.

I'm forty-five years old and I have nothing.

We're riding the Third Street bus. The show is way the hell out in Hunters Point—one of San Francisco's worst neighborhoods—and the club is owned and operated by the Hells Angels. There's going to be alcohol and drugs, and plenty of non-recovery type substances and sketchy behaviors. In the 12 Step nomenclature, this is known as a "slippery place" where the addict/alcoholic has no control over "people, places, or things" and because they have put themselves in this situation they are in danger of relapsing, which is also reason enough to get kicked out of rehab.

The bus pulls up to our stop and we get off. We're on the backside of Hunters Point. A no man's land where the industrial area stops and the housing projects begin. The club is somewhere down Cargo Way, a dark, unlit street that meanders off towards the old Navy shipyard.

This is the Kennedys' first show in San Francisco without Biafra. Ray, Klaus and D.H. had recently reformed the band with Brandon Cruz, the singer from Dr. Know, and now after years of inactivity they're about to start touring again. I'd been in touch with Microwave, and he'd put me on the guest list with a plus one. Only I hadn't realized it'd be out here, in the middle of nowhere. I don't own a car. Hell, I don't own shit. I'm in rehab.

Eventually, I do relapse and piss dirty for my parole officer. Before he can violate my parole, I put myself in rehab. When he finally catches up with me, I've been in treatment for over a month. He tells me as long as I stay there he'd forget everything and let me be.

There's no bus going our direction. George and I start walking. The road is deserted. It's absolutely desolate. Fields full of weeds, abandoned stripped cars, derelict buildings, and piles of garbage surround us. Off in the distance, there's a huge tower for a cement factory. Even farther out are the lights of ships moored in the Bay.

A car careens down a side road and fishtails across the intersection, narrowly missing us in the crosswalk. An old man, his speech incoherent, leans out the window and cusses us out. I'm beginning to think this isn't such a good idea. I'm nervous when a passing pickup truck honks his horn. "Hey, punkers. Where ya headed?" Microwave pulls over to the side of the road. We gratefully jump in the truck.

The club, a small, square cinderblock building with a fenced-in parking lot, sits at the end of the road. It looks like some obscure roadhouse, not exactly the kind of place one normally associates with a punk show, and definitely not the usual San Francisco venue.

The inside is just as dismal. There's a small stage, an okay PA, and a bar that also offers food. The maximum capacity is maybe five hundred. There are a lot of underage kids.

I run into Ray and Klaus. They introduce me to Brandon. We're standing around talking. I miss these guys. It's been way too long since I've seen them. It's been years since I was on tour, and memories of being on the road and working for the band feel overwhelming.

"Got a road crew?" I ask Ray.

"Yeah, we hired some people." Ray is hesitant in his response. I realize it must sound like I'm asking for my old job back, which is a fucking joke.

"Cool," I say, trying to relieve the awkwardness hanging in the air.

The opening band starts and the club is so small there's nowhere to get away from the noise except outside in the smoking area. Everyone breaks off in different directions, and George and I are left standing in the middle of the room. I feel totally out of place. It's been years since I've been inside a club. I don't know what to do. I've always been working when I was at a show. But, I'm not part of the crew. I don't have access to the dressing room backstage. After a few minutes, I wander outside to the smoking area.

I'm stressed out, chain smoking cigarettes. D.H. is talking with Warner from The Sick. I nod to him. He ignores me. A bunch of drug addict bullshit from the past transpired between us and I worry he's still holding it against me.

Everyone is drinking and talking and hanging out, having what appears to be a good time. I'm self-conscious. This is so awkward. I shouldn't have come. I'm not ready to be at a bar. I'm not ready to try and act like everything is okay. I'm not who I used to be. I haven't been that person in a very long time. I'm an ex-con bank-robber. Now I'm in rehab. I have no idea what I'm supposed to do. All I know is it's hard as hell living without heroin and, being here, it's becoming more and more obvious that time has passed me by. So much has changed. I can't just instantly resume where I left off fifteen years ago.

"Let's get the fuck outta here."

"But the Kennedys haven't played."

"They played a long time ago."

AUTHOR'S NOTE

There have been times in my life when I was done. I was tired of living. I was haunted by my past, the present was hell, and the future looked even bleaker. Yet the times depicted in this book are when most of that wasn't happening. Of course, there were difficulties, hard moments, and severe losses, but on a whole, the years I was on the road I was happy, the drugs were "working," and music was everything. For all the ups and downs and deaths and failures, there was laughter, success, love, friendships, passion, and, most of all, community. And I like to think I've captured some of that here. But because this book is about what really happened, there's going to be contrary responses. There's fear of the truth. There's anger when people realize this is who we truly were. And there's disbelief and rejection from those who remember differently. Yet the reality is that what's in this book is what I remember. These are my memories. Not yours. Not what someone told me. Not shit I made up. You want to dispute what I've written? Then go write your own damn book. You want to hate me for telling the truth? Stand in line behind me, because I have enough self-hatred for all of us. You want to critique me for being a fucked up human being? You are years too late. But if you want to read a book that lets you into my world, my memories, and what I experienced—you're in the right place.

ACKNOWLEDGEMENTS

A big heartfelt thank you to one and all. Whether you know it or not, you kept me sane and helped bring this book to life.

Special thanks to Iris Berry and Punk Hostage Press for giving my book a home and welcoming me into the PHP family.

A debt of gratitude to Rob Roberge, Craig Clevenger, Jillian Lauren, Bernadette Murphy, and Josh Indar for reading the shitty first drafts and kicking down the much-needed notes and critiques in order to make it better.

To my immediate family: Jenn, Jagger, and Mercer. Thank you for putting up with my "creative process"—which basically means dealing with my anxiety and depression on a daily basis.

A shout out to the Origami Pancake Crew for no other reason than I'm stoked that you all are who you are.

A big thank you to Todd Taylor over at Razorcake for cleaning up the mess.

And finally to everyone whose lives and deeds made the telling of this book possible (and if I've left you out it wasn't on purpose): Chris Grayson (RIP), Will Shatter (RIP), D.H. Peligro, 4-Way, Michael Bonanno, Tracy Chick (RIP), Klaus Fluoride, East Bay Ray, Mike Roche, Ron Emory, Jack Grisham, Scott O'Neil, Neil Kraft, Mia d'Bruzzi, Robert "Indian" Bergman, Gerry Hurtado (RIP), Jimmy Crucifix, Eric Borst, Paul Casteel, John Marsh (RIP), K.O., Susan Miller, Anna Lisa Van der Valk, Bo Sweeting (RIP), Patti Ramelli (RIP), Debbie Gordon, Danny Roman (RIP), Gary Floyd, Deanne Franklin, Emilio Crixell, John Surrell, Deanna Mitchell, Cecilia Kuhn (RIP), Winston Smith, Bruno De Smartass, Ted

Falconi, Mike Vraney (RIP), Chester Simpson, Jeff Good (RIP), Bob Clic, Ruby Ray, Paul Zahl, Stanley Greene (RIP), Arab, Mark Johnson, Stan Lee, Gary Tovar, Kevin Lyman, Dirk Dirkson (RIP), Ginger Coyote, Bill Miller, Chris Crud, Michelle Rebel, Denise Ondayko, Dick Lucas, Bruce Treasure, Phil Bryant, Trotsky, Pete-the-Roadie, Joe Wood, Michael Reidy (and all the folks at the S.F. Punk Rock Sewing Circle), Kathy Peck, Violet Levy, Chris Kross, Ward Abronski, Bruce Lose, Jimmy Wilsey (RIP), Melissa McChesney (RIP), Dave Rat, Karrie Keyes, and yes, even you Eric Boucher.

MORE ABOUT ANARCHY AT THE CIRCLE K

Anarchy at the Circle K is a bittersweet series of adventures brilliantly described by "our hero" in the role of roadie slash drug and sex fiend during punk's hardcore era. Patrick O'Neil survives to tell of his descent into the dregs of bottomless addiction and subsequent redemption in this true-life, enjoyable, often uncomfortable, hilarious, and highly recommended read.
    —Danny Furious, Avengers

A tour de force of the punk rock scene written by a man who lived it, *Anarchy at the Circle K* is a wild ride from page one to the last. A book that takes off fast and never lets up, crisscrossing the country in an insane, violent, and tumultuous tour of drugs, booze, sex, and rock and roll. With a passion for the music and the dangers that came with it, Patrick O'Neil has written a remarkable, firsthand account of life on the road with some of America's greatest punk rock bands. Ex-roadie, ex-heroin addict, ex-con, O'Neil is hard and tough and calls it like he sees it, never pulling his punches, a fearless truth-teller who's earned his place among the very best of L.A.'s grittiest writers. What a fine and powerful book.
    —James Brown, author of *The Los Angeles Diaries*

Anarchy at the Circle K pulses with the kinetic urgency of the best road novels, and with the wisdom, vulnerability, and hard-won truths of the finest memoirs. This is one of the best from one of the finest writers working today.
    —Rob Roberge, The Urinals

Patrick O'Neil's *Anarchy at the Circle K* takes us all over Reagan-era America, from one shithole venue to the next, capturing the grueling grind of DIY punk tours, the endless, desperate quest for drugs, and countless run-ins with the law. Written at the relentless pace of a good hardcore show, the book is equal parts thrilling, raw, insane, and surprisingly touching. Dead Kennedys, Flipper, Subhumans, and T.S.O.L. figure prominently in the narrative but, ultimately, it's O'Neil's unique perspective from the eye of the punk cultural hurricane that makes the book impossible to put down.

—Michael Stewart Foley, author of the 33 1/3 book on Dead Kennedys' *Fresh Fruit for Rotting Vegetables*

MORE ABOUT THE AUTHOR

Patrick O'Neil is a former junkie bank robber and the author of the memoirs *Gun, Needle, Spoon* and *Hold-Up*. He is the co-author of two instructional writing manuals, *Writing Your Way to Recovery: How Stories Can Save Our Lives* (with the author James Brown) and the PEN America Prison Writing Handbook, *The Sentences that Create Us: Crafting a Writer's Life in Prison*." In the early '80s he was a roadie and/or road manager for Dead Kennedys, Flipper, T.S.O.L., Subhumans, and The Dickies. He worked stage for the Mabuhay Gardens, the On Broadway, and Goldenvoice. And he was fired from the first Lollapalooza tour for being "too loaded." After years of heroin addiction, he turned to crime to support his habit, got busted, and was convicted of two counts of armed robbery. Getting clean off drugs in 2001, he started working as a drug and alcohol counselor. In 2015, the State of California granted him a Certificate of Rehabilitation. In 2016, California Governor Edmund G. Brown awarded him a governor's pardon. O'Neil holds an MFA in creative writing from Antioch University Los Angeles. He has taught writing workshops in numerous correctional facilities, universities, and institutions, and continues to work for prison reform. He currently resides in Los Angeles with his wife Jennifer, a Maine Coon named Jagger, and a squirrel named Mercer.

Photo by Jennifer Courtney

MORE BOOKS ON PUNK HOSTAGE PRESS

Danny Baker
> *Fractured* - 2012

A Razor
> *Better Than a Gun in A Knife* Fight - 2012
> *Drawn Blood: Collected Works*
> *From D.B.P.LTD., 1985-1995* - 2012
> *Beaten Up Beaten Down* - 2012
> *Small Catastrophes in A Big World* - 2012
> *Half- Century Status* - 2013
> *Days of Xmas Poems* - 2014
> *Puro Purismo* - 2021

Iris Berry
> *The Daughters of Bastards* - 2012
> *All That Shines Under the Hollywood Sign* – 2019
> *The Trouble With Palm Trees* - 2021
> *Gas Station Etiquette* - 2022

C.V. Auchterlonie
> *Impress* - 2012

Yvonne De la Vega
> *Tomorrow, Yvonne - Poetry & Prose for Suicidal Egoists* - 2012

Carolyn Srygley- Moore
> *Miracles Of the Blog: A Series* - 2012

Rich Ferguson
> 8th & Agony -2012

Jack Grisham
> *Untamed* -2013
> *Code Blue: A Love Story* ~ Limited Edition—2014
> *Pulse of the World. Arthur Chance, Punk Rock Detective* - 2022

Dennis Cruz
> *Moth Wing Tea* - 2013
> *The Beast Is We* - 2018

Frank Reardon
> *Blood Music* - 2013

Pleasant Gehman
> *Showgirl Confidential*—2013
> *Rock 'N' Roll Witch: A Memoir of Sex Magick, Drugs, And Rock 'N' Roll* - 2022

Hollie Hardy
> *How To Take a Bullet and Other Survival Poems*—2014

MORE BOOKS ON PUNK HOSTAGE PRESS

Made in the USA
Columbia, SC
05 October 2022

68600472R20155